Overcoming the Barriers to
Higher Education

Overcoming the Barriers to Higher Education

Stephen Gorard
with Nick Adnett, Helen May, Kim Slack,
Emma Smith and Liz Thomas

Trentham Books
Stoke on Trent, UK and Sterling, USA

Trentham Books Limited
Westview House   22883 Quicksilver Drive
734 London Road   Sterling
Oakhill   VA 20166-2012
Stoke on Trent   USA
Staffordshire
England ST4 5NP

First published 2007

British Library Cataloguing-in-Publication Data
A catalogue record for this book is available from the
British Library

ISBN: 978-1-85856-414-2

Designed and typeset by Trentham Print Design Ltd., Chester and
printed in Great Britain by Hobbs the Printers Ltd, Hampshire.

Contents

List of tables

List of figures

Abbreviations

AGCAS   Association of Graduate Careers Advisory Services

ALG   Assembly Learning Grants

AP(E)L   Accreditation of Prior (experiential) Learning

API   Age Participation Index

APL   Accreditation of Prior Learning

BCS   British Cohort Study

DfEE   Department for Education and Employment

DFES   Department for Education and Skills

ETAG   Education and Training Action Group

EU   European Union

FCF   Financial Contingency Fund

FE   Further Education

FEI   Further Education Institution

GDP   Gross Domestic Product

GCSE   General Certificate of Secondary Education

GIS   Geographic Information Systems

GNVQ   General National Vocational Qualification

HE   Higher Education

HECS   Higher Education Contribution Scheme

HEFCE   Higher Education Funding Council for England

HEFCW Higher Education Funding Council for Wales

HEI   Higher Education Institution

HESA   Higher Education Statistics Agency

HNC   Higher National Certificate

HND	Higher National Diploma
ICT	Information Communication Technology
ISR	Individual Student Record
IT	Information Technology
LEAPS	Lothian Equal Access Programme
NACETT	National Advisory Council for Education and Training Targets
NCDS	National Child Development Study
NEET	Not in education, employment or training
NIACE	National Institute of Adult Continuing Education
NPC	National Postgraduate Committee
NQF	National Qualification Framework
NVQ	National Vocational Qualification
OECD	Organisation for Economic Cooperation and Development
OFFA	Office for Fair Access
PRR	Participation Rate Ratio
SES	Socio-economic status
SWAP	Scottish Wider Access Programme
UCAS	Universities and Colleges Admissions Service
UK	United Kingdom
US	United States
UUK	Universities UK
WP	Widening Participation
YCS	Youth Cohort Study

Preface

In 2004, the Higher Education Funding Council for England (HEFCE) commissioned this team of authors, then at the Universities of York and Staffordshire and from the Higher Education Academy, to conduct an independent review of the existing relevant evidence on widening participation in HE, with particular reference to the varied barriers faced by potential and actual students. This book is an updated summary of the evidence we uncovered and of the substantive conclusions that can be drawn from it.

The authors would like to acknowledge the assistance of Jonathan Gorard, Beng Huat See, Chris Taylor and Stephanie Tierney in the preparation of some of the material presented here.

Introduction

1

Higher education and the problem of access

This is a book about higher education (HE), about the experiences of people who take part in HE and the reasons why many other people do not take part. In this introductory chapter we describe briefly what HE is, and how the problem of widening access to HE has become a key policy issue in the UK and in many developed and developing countries. We then explain how the remainder of the book is structured. It summarises the available research evidence on these issues and makes practical recommendations concerning the problem of unfairness in patterns of access to HE for different social and economic groups.

What is higher education?

Internationally, Wikipedia (2006) defines HE as: 'education provided by universities and other institutions that award academic degrees', but adds that 'most professional education is included within higher education, and many postgraduate qualifications are strongly vocationally or professionally oriented.'

HE is defined by the Higher Education Funding Council for England (HEFCE, 2006) in the glossary on their home pages, as:

> ... courses generally above the standard of GCE A-levels or National Vocational Qualification (NVQ) Level 3. They include degree courses, postgraduate courses and Higher National Diplomas. Higher education takes place in universities and higher education colleges, and in some further education colleges.

Prospects (2002) similarly defines HE as 'all courses of one year or more, above A-level and its equivalents, that lead to a qualification awarded by higher education institutions or widely recognised national awarding bodies'. We recognise each of these as describing HE for the purposes of this book. Our main focus, though, is on undergraduate courses and provision at level 4 of the UK National Qualification Framework (NQF), or its equivalent.

Patterns of post-compulsory participation

A successful learning society would be one in which everyone obtains high quality general education, leading to a comprehensive post-school education and training system in which everyone has access to suitable opportunities for life-long learning, including a university within geographical reach of everyone (Coffield, 1997). Within this society, provision of education would be both excellent and fair, leading to individual learning, national economic prosperity and social integration (Quicke, 1997). Mass participation in such a system is seen by some as necessary to provide a fulfilled life for individuals, a successful and developing economy and a genuinely participative democracy (NIACE, 1994), while equal opportunities in learning are a precursor to equality of opportunity in employment and citizenship (FEU, 1993). Although it remains a disputed notion, this is a fair summary of what the 'learning society' is deemed to be in British official discourse (Brown and Lauder, 1996; Otterson, 2004).

Yet inequalities in participation in all forms of post-compulsory education have endured over the past 50 years in the UK with significant minorities routinely excluded (Pettigrew *et al*, 1989; DfEE, 1995; Beinart and Smith, 1998). Over a third of the adult population have not participated in any formal episodes of learning at all since reaching school leaving age (Gorard and Rees, 2002; NIACE, 2003). Those individuals who do participate in post-compulsory education are heavily patterned by pre-adult social, geographic and historical factors such as socio-economic status, year of birth and type of school attended. All relevant research studies over decades, using whatever approach, attest to these inequalities (Sargant and Aldridge, 2002). Participation in post-compulsory education and training opportunities in England has long been markedly differentiated in terms of socio-economic groups (Bynner, 1992; Marsh and Blackburn, 1992; Macleod and Lambe, 2006). Sargant (2000) points out that a number of large scale studies such as those from Glass (1954) to Gorard *et al* (1999a) have shown these patterns and that the determinants of participation, far from being easily fixable, are long-term, and rooted in family, locality and history. The situation is the same or worse across the EU (European Group for Research on Equity in Educational Systems, 2005). Indeed, some recent figures suggest that these patterns of exclusion are growing (Kingston, 2004). We know that those currently disenfranchised from formal and non-formal adult education and training (the non-learners) are more frequently not employed and are older, with lower literacy skills or with negative attitudes to institutional learning. In general individuals from families with less prestigious occupational backgrounds, with lower incomes, the unemployed or economically inactive, the elderly, severely disabled people and ex-offenders are less likely than average to participate in any episodes of formal education or training after the age of 16.

Recent work has also emphasised the role of regional influences in determining patterns of participation (Selwyn *et al*, 2006). Because the individual characteristics underlying these patterns of participation are not evenly distributed across the country, participation is also patterned by place of residence, leading to different rates of participation in different areas and regions of the UK (HEFCE, 2005). These inequalities are perpetuated by the fact that those who participate and benefit most from adult learning tend to be those who have higher educational attainment levels already and who continue learning throughout their life (OECD, 2003). Those who are already better educated or qualified and more likely to be in work and employed at a higher grade are also more likely to receive subsequent work-related training. This may be because their educational record is seen as providing evidence that they are trainable (Banks *et al*, 1992; McGivney, 1993). For example, in one study, only 3 per cent of those who left school at the minimum age reported taking part in any education or training in the past three years, compared with 65 per cent of those who continued in initial education beyond the minimum age (Park, 1994).

This means that post-compulsory participation in education becomes a lifelong pattern for some, while non-participation becomes an alternative lifelong pattern for others. How does participation in HE fit into this overall picture of stratified access to post-compulsory education?

The problem of access to HE

Participation in HE by students aged 17 to 30 in England in 2004/05 was around 42 per cent, a slight fall from 2003 and a slightly larger fall from 2002 (THES, 2006). Current government policy is to increase HE participation in England to 50 per cent of those aged between 18 and 30 by the year 2010. Originally this 50 per cent target was expressed as the sum of the percentages of students entering HE for the first time (Prospects, 2002) but it now refers to

3

those still in HE after six months (Prospects, 2005). The pressure to increase participation is intended to be directed primarily at those groups who were previously under-represented, especially students from low income families and low-participation regions. The current student body is highly stratified in terms of class, ethnicity, and location – just as it is in post-compulsory education more generally, and perhaps even more so. The government has spent at least £2 billion on widening participation (WP) activities since 1997 and despite this there has been a reported fall in the percentage of young entrants from lower social classes (Sanders, 2006). This shows what a difficult task WP is.

The terms 'access' and 'widening participation' are in common use but they do not have a clear or shared meaning. For example, widening participation has been interpreted by some as increasing student numbers or recruiting more students from state schools, whereas a stronger equity focus would ensure that it was about greater access for students from groups that are under-represented in HE in comparison to their population share (see Chapter Three). This widening – as distinct from merely increasing – participation agenda is predicated on the notion that particular social groups, defined by social class or ethnic background, are unfairly under-represented in higher education. Taking post-compulsory education and training as a totality, opportunities of some sort are available to the entire adult population. These include library drop-in centres, free basic skills provision, jobseeker training, liberal evening classes and courses delivered entirely by technologies such as television or computer. Therefore, the continued under-representation of certain groups in these objectively open episodes suggests a pervading problem (Gorard and Rees, 2002). However, unlike the patterns in life-long learning more generally, it is not clear that this unfair under-representation in HE has been established – and for a very simple reason.

HE, defined by some as a post A-level learning opportunity, was initially not intended to be available to all and is largely based on selective entry in a way which other life-long educational opportunities are not. The majority of first places at HE institutions in England are allocated on the basis of applicants' prior qualifications. Therefore, we need to consider how these are generated. If the prior qualifications are distributed as unevenly as the opportunities for HE then this both explains the patterns of participation in HE and also suggests that using prior qualifications in this way may be unfair.

We cannot therefore consider widening HE participation without a more detailed consideration of who these additional participants are intended to be. Is HE participation lower in less affluent areas because of poverty of aspiration among the relevant age cohorts? Or is it the generally lower initial school qualifications in poorer areas that precede and largely determine the lower level of participation? The answer is crucial for policy purposes but this issue is rarely addressed directly with even tentative figures. If the former explanation is true then policies to persuade children from families in poverty of the benefits of HE such as means-tested grants and interest-free loans are appropriate. If the latter explanation is true then such policies can have only limited effects because their client base is so small. In this case a much greater emphasis needs to be put into strategies to prepare students of all ages for pre-university qualifications and to ameliorate the position of the under-privileged in society. These issues are central to the concerns of this book.

The structure of the book

Chapter Two outlines the characteristics and flaws of the large scale datasets available to UK analysts calculating patterns of participation in HE and Chapter Three uses these datasets to consider which students are missing from, or under-represented in, HE. Chapter Four briefly reviews the range and quality of existing research evidence available to policy makers and practitioners working in widening participation (WP), and highlights some of the issues involved in attempting a synthesis of evidence as wide and varied as appears in this book. Chapters Five and Six begin our life-course summary by considering the available evidence on the trajectory of individuals from birth to their possible transition to higher education. Chapters Seven and Eight look at the initial experiences of learners in HE and what can be done to encourage and retain those likely to drop out. Chapter Nine considers the destinations and careers of graduates as possible motivators or barriers to undergraduate participation. Chapter Ten summarises the findings from the book, and the practical lessons learned for those concerned with overcoming the barriers to participation.

2

Assessing the patterns of inequality in higher education

Introduction

In Chapter One, we explained that our concern is with preventing the unfair denial of HE to some sections of society in the UK, leading to the unfair under-representation of certain social groups in HE. In order to establish that access to higher education is actually unfair we need to demonstrate that particular social groups are seriously under-represented in universities, and that this has no reasonable or merited explanation. In a sense, this sounds easy to demonstrate but it is dependent on a sequence of less than perfect analytical steps (Gorard and Smith, 2006) which include having:

- a suitable definition of, and method of measuring membership of the social groups involved

- a suitable definition and characterisation of the relevant population

- an accurate measure of the prevalence of the social groups in the relevant population

- an agreed definition of what we mean by participation in HE

- an accurate measure of the prevalence of those with higher education experience in the social groups involved

From the results of these five steps, we can calculate the difference between the proportion of each social group in the relevant population and the proportion of the same group in HE. If this difference is large and important then we can assume that there is a problem requiring explanation and amelioration. This, in essence, should form the basis for the HE widening participation agenda in England and Wales.

Defining social categories

To establish that there should be more of a particular social group in HE than there is we first need to define the group clearly, so that the definition could be used by different people in different places at different times to mean the same thing. Unfortunately, the categorisation of social groups by occupational class or ethnicity is a matter of judgement over which even experts disagree (Lambert, 2002; Lee, 2003). The categories themselves are somewhat arbitrary (Gorard, 2003). A key problem in examining trends in social categories over time is that the variables collected, or the coding used for the same variables, also change. So it is often difficult to make genuine and straightforward comparisons over time or between groups. This is true of the Higher Education Statistic Agency (HESA) datasets which record the ethnic origin of students in HE. Until 2001/02 there was only one category for white students in the UK. Now a distinction has been made between white, white-British, white-Irish, white-Scottish, Irish traveller and other white. There are now, also, categories for a number of mixed ethnic groups, including mixed white. Whilst this may reflect changes in society and could increase the completion rate by students asked to state their ethnicity, it makes comparison over time more difficult.

There have also been moves away from classifying the occupational backgrounds of students in terms of skill or prestige. The significance of the categories themselves, such as the meaning attached to being in a non-manual occupation, changes with their prevalence and through historical/economic development. Significantly for the measurement of WP, it is not clear whether the classification by ethnicity or occupation should be of the potential student or of their parents. For example, it seems absurd to try and base the occupational classification of a student on their own work history when they may never have been anything other a full-time student in education. But where the occupations of the two parents differ, which is to be preferred? If one or more of the parents has not lived with the student, does this make a difference? It is no less absurd to base the occupational classification of a student aged 45 on the previous occupation of their parents. If, on the other hand, we use two different classification systems for younger and older students, when should the cut-off point be? Should the cut-off be based on age alone or on work experience? Can we reasonably aggregate the classifications based on the two different systems?

As we shall illustrate repeatedly in this chapter there is no simple answer to these analytical questions. Yet every analysis covering patterns of participation must make, even by default, a bewildering number of these decisions and every analyst might quite reasonably make a different set of decisions. Unless these analytical compromises are clearly reported there is a danger that debates about what is happening in widening participation will be misinterpreted by commentators as being about issues of substance whereas they are merely about differences in analytical decisions.

Defining the relevant population

The next step in establishing that there should be more of a particular social group in HE requires us to assess the prevalence of that social group in the relevant population. Unfortunately, when researching episodes of post-compulsory learning it is not clear what the relevant population is. An analyst using figures for all adults is open to the charge that the inclusion of people over the age of 50 is irrelevant since so few of these are currently participating in HE, even though this represents a large proportion of the population. An analyst using only young adults, however, is open to the charge of presuming that WP is only about traditional-age students and so excluding from the analysis precisely those to whom access could and should be widened. It is not even clear what is the youngest age that should be considered in the population of potential HE students. Some higher education institutions (HEIs) admit students at age 16 or even younger on rare occasions. This decision about age is crucial to our results because the characteristics of the population of England have changed over time in terms of the prevalence of ethnic and occupational groups. Using population figures for all ages may lead one analyst to conclude that working-class students are under-represented, while an ethnic minority is over-represented in HE. Another analyst, using the same figures for HE but using population figures only for those aged 17-21, may conclude the reverse. The opposite conclusion can be drawn from the same HE data by different analysts because the proportion of working-class families may have been decreasing over time in England, while the proportion of an ethnic minority group may have been increasing.

A similarly key decision for an analysis of participation patterns in one country concerns the original domicile of the potential students. In an analysis for England, is only the population of England relevant or should the analysis include the potential students, and so the population of the other home countries of the UK – Scotland, Wales and Northern Ireland? Excluding them complicates the analysis because it is then essential to distinguish

England-domiciled students from others. But as with the definition of social categories, this leads to issues about whose domicile counts. Is it the residence of parents, of the potential students themselves or some combination of these? Students from within the European Union are treated and charged fees as home students. Does this mean that the populations of all EU countries must also be in the analysis? This leads to several analytic problems, most notably that the population of countries like the Czech Republic is different from England. So, even if comparable official population figures from the Czech Republic exist, and this is unlikely, it means that the population figures in our analysis will be considerably affected by those of a country which provides an almost negligible proportion of students for HE in England.

Measuring the characteristics of the population

If an analytical decision has been made to exclude overseas applicants, then the population census of the UK provides the most complete coverage to assess the characteristics of the relevant population. But this census only happens every ten years, and some of the most relevant questions for this analysis are only asked of a sub-sample of 10 per cent of the cases. Even so, and despite it being a legal requirement, not every household takes part, not everyone is in a household and not everyone who takes part responds to the class and ethnicity questions even when asked them. The categories used for the class and ethnicity questions are not the same between years such as 1991 and 2001, nor are they always the same as those used in other large data sets – such as the individualised student records (ISRs) held by the Higher Education Statistics Agency (HESA) for all students, the Universities and Colleges Admissions Service (UCAS) database of applicants or the annual schools' census. This makes it difficult to track trends over time and to use the population figures as the denominator in the final step of this analysis.

The annual schools' census does not ask for parental occupation and the most commonly-used indicator of disadvantage that it provides instead is eligibility for free school meals, which is not recorded for applicants to HE. The UCAS figures for entry qualification to HE exclude the majority of each age cohort who do not apply to HE. Therefore it is not possible to compare directly the qualifications attained at school by different social classes with the rates of participation in HE. We can only estimate the relevant figures from sample surveys, often with high non-response or longitudinal dropout and sometimes with incompatible measures of class or qualification. Coupled with the many cases in HE which are not classified by occupation the situation for analysis is highly unsatisfactory. Yet it must be stressed that this is the best kind of evidence available for studies of widening participation.

Defining participation in HE

For the fourth step in our apparently simple but increasingly complex calculation, we next need to know the prevalence of the social group that had participated in HE. This step also faces problems of yet more crucial analytical decisions that could swing the results of the analysis either way. We need to know what proportion of the population has already participated in HE even if they did not receive a qualification. We need to decide whether to include NQF level 4 (HE) courses in FE colleges, level 3 (pre-HE) courses in HE institutions, postgraduate or level 5 students, those involved in professional training such as postgraduate teachers and social workers, or those involved in short courses such as HE-based continuing professional development. Do we include those taking degrees by correspondence or via the internet? We need to know whether we distinguish between England, UK, Commonwealth, and EU home students. If not, then our prior population figures become more problematic. If so, then some datasets make it difficult to distinguish between categories of home students. Any variation in these decisions over time or between analysts makes comparisons between their results difficult. As with the general population figures, HE records are incomplete and for some years of the data the Individualised Student Records (ISRs) are not linked to individuals but to courses, so that a part-time student taking two courses in two different institutions does not have a unique identifier and is in danger of being counted twice (Gorard and Taylor, 2001).

Measuring the characteristics of those in HE

The final requirement, before being able to make the relatively simple arithmetic calculation involved in producing the proportionate representation of social groups in HE, is in some ways the easiest since it concerns only those in HE. However, we shall spend some time explaining difficulties in using the data even for this group to help readers understand the severe limitations of our own analysis of patterns of participation in Chapter Three. There are no ideal datasets for the analysis of patterns of participation in higher education (HE) in terms of policy changes, or social, economic, or regional disparities. All existing datasets suffer from one or more defects: they include only participants, have incomplete coverage, have substantial proportions of missing data or cases, have changed key definitions over time or are incompatible in range or aggregation with other datasets.

Missing cases

As with the population Census, there are cases simply missing from official statistics on participation in HE and as with the population Census we cannot be entirely sure how many cases are missing. The UCAS data on applicants to HE has historically seriously under-represented part-time, mature and distance students. Returns from university of students in place may give a better indication of the overall figures but are generally deficient in terms of key background variables such as ethnicity and occupational class.

Missing responses

An even more common problem for the relevant large scale datasets lies in data missing even from existing cases. For example, many of the variables in the Higher Education Statistics Agency (HESA) datasets are compulsory; some value has to be reported for each student. But this does not mean that complete data are available for every student. The missing data, which can include not known, information refused, information not yet sought, and other non-completed often covers a large proportion of the students. One example is that other than 'white', 'missing' is officially the largest ethnic group among students in England. In fact, the unknown cases considerably outnumber all the ethnic minority groups combined. Some of the ethnic minority groups are quite small, meaning that very small changes in their absolute numbers can make trends over time or differences between groups appear more volatile than they really are. The high proportion of missing cases in an analysis using this variable could significantly bias the results being presented, even where the overall response rate is high. This means that any differences over time and place or between social groups needs to be robust enough to overcome this bias amongst many others. The scale of a difference or change must be such that it dwarfs the bias introduced by measurement errors, missing cases and changes in data collection methods over time. This is seldom acknowledged by commentators or analysts.

Similarly, UCAS applicant figures and HESA ISRs have a large proportion of cases with no occupational category. In fact, when non-responses are added to those cases which are unclassifiable by occupation (through being economically inactive, for example) then having no occupational category becomes the single largest classification. In 2002/2003 45 per cent of first year undergraduates were unclassifiable in terms of occupational background according to HESA figures. Mayhew *et al,* (2004) present an analysis of participation by social class using UCAS figures, in which 30 per cent of students are occupationally unclassified. With this number of missing number cases, small differences between groups or changes over time should be ignored.

Some studies have attempted to overcome these limitations by using postal code data with Geographic Information Systems (GIS). However, it is not clear that this helps at all. These analyses are still limited by the incompleteness of the census. There is the added problem of the availability and accuracy of the home post codes of students. For example, only 47 per cent of Welsh-domiciled students in 2002/03 had valid postcodes (Taylor and Gorard, 2005) and even this figure depends on some contestable assumptions about the nature of domicile. And analysts are still faced by the fact that they are using GIS so that they can associate individuals with the average background characteristics of the area in which they live. Students are thus assumed to have the same occupational background as the modal category in the area. If the area is small, then the results are more affected by patterns of missing data. If the area is large, then the modal category may not do justice to the variability of the measure. Whether this approach improves the quality of analysis is therefore debatable.

Missing variables

A final consideration in the context of missing data involves missing variables. This is one of the most important and least reported types of missing data because the researcher is often unaware of it. This goes far beyond the omitted variable bias discussed in econometric models. To illustrate the way in which missing variables can affect the conclusions of research, consider the following example. The Higher Education Funding Council for England (HEFCE, 2005) reports that around 30 per cent of young people in England go to HE and that participation is higher in Scotland. It also reports that a higher proportion of HE participants in England are enrolled in HEIs than in Scotland. In Scotland, students studying at HE level while enrolled in Further Education Institutions (FEIs) are more common. The report (HEFCE, 2005) then attributes the higher participation in Scotland to the greater use of FE for HE purposes, making a direct causal claim. The Executive Summary states:

> In Scotland this is not the case: around a third of young entrants study HE courses in further education institutions (FEIs), which *helps to make* Scotland's participation rate some 9 percentage points higher than England's. HEFCE (2005, p5)

HEFCE should have considered a more plausible explanation first. Levels of prior attainment at level 3 are also higher in Scotland, meaning that we should expect higher HE participation there because entry to HE is so heavily predicated on prior qualifications. Hutton (2005) compares an analysis of participation in HE that does not take prior qualifications into account to an analysis of regional patterns of lung cancer that did not take patterns of smoking into account. Yet, this approach is common because existing data-sets on qualifications from initial education do not link with individual student records from FE and HE.

Difficulties of analysis

The analysis required to produce patterns of participation in HE by social groups is relatively simple once the preceding analytic decisions and necessary compromises have been made. For example, the proportion of the social group under consideration – such as an ethnic minority – can be compared in HE and in the relevant population by dividing the former by the latter. A result of one (1) shows proportionate participation and a figure less than one (<1) shows under-representation. Whether such under-representation should be assumed to be unfair is discussed later in the book. In the final section of this chapter we consider how far above or below one the final figure must be to merit explanation, and look at judging differences in participation over time.

When evaluating the impact of change in policy or practice by looking at changes over time in participation it is essential to take a long-term perspective. Otherwise a regular annual increase in any measure can be misguidedly attributed to a specific policy, as frequently happens with the annual increase in GCSE and A-level scores. It is also important to distinguish between at least two different kinds of change when looking at changes over time. The first is historical change over time which affects successive cohorts of learners. This is the kind of change that policy interventions are intended to bring about, but which also happens due to longer-term social and economic change. The second is a change in the life of each individual learner, such as a decision whether to participate in an educational opportunity. In the aggregate these two kinds of change can look very similar and so lead to considerable confusion about the meaning of evidence for the unwary observer. For example, Gorard *et al*, (2002a, 2002b) show that the impact of the setting up and monitoring of targets for life-long learning in England and Wales has been widely misunderstood. These targets have a common structure such as:

> By [year], [percentage] of working-age adults will have attained [qualification level] – or will have participated in [educational opportunity].

For example, ETAG (1999) produced the following target for Wales:

> The proportion of adults of working age with an NVQ level 2 or equivalent to increase from over 5 in 10 in 1996 to 7 in 10 by 2002 and over 7 in 10 by 2004.

Working age here was defined for males as aged 16-64, and for females as aged 16-59.

Every year the percentage of the working-age population with any level of qualification such as NQF level 2 or equivalent increases. This has been heralded as a success for various adult learning interventions including the setting of targets (NACETT, 1994). The implication is that adult education has improved. However, this conclusion ignores the factor of historical change when making claims about individual learning. In England and Wales the percentage of 16-year-olds attaining a NQF level 2 qualification at school (equivalent to 5 high grade GCSEs) is much higher than the percentage of retirees at age 60/65 with the equivalent qualification. Every year, another cohort of relatively highly qualified individuals enters the official definition of 'working-age' and another cohort of relatively poorly qualified retirees leaves it. Some progress towards the target is made automatically each year without a single adult having to gain a qualification after the age of 16. This 'conveyor belt effect' must be taken into account before we can claim evidence of a positive change in adult learning since the introduction of targets.

Although not always as obvious as this, confusion between historical and life time changes is widespread in the WP literature. One way of overcoming the problem is to use data from separate cohorts and examine only the changes that occur over the life of each cohort, but to draw comparisons between different historical cohorts. Unfortunately cohort studies of this kind are even rarer than the ten year population census and they exacerbate one of the other generic deficits of the datasets available for WP conclusions: the absence of substantial amounts of the relevant data. A typical cohort study like the 1970 Birth Cohort Study (BCS) uses a group of neonates and seeks permission to follow them through their lives. The study started with 16,695 cases in Britain. By 1999, 2,608 were untraced, 246 confirmed emigrated, 109 died, and 338 refused, leaving 13,394 cases (Bynner et al, 2000, p31). Unfortunately, the cases dropping out at each 'sweep' are not random, so introducing a substantial bias for subsequent analysis. Although this potential for bias should be highlighted and taken into account by analysts and their users, this is not always the case.

A study by Blanden et al (2005) is having considerable impact in the UK, appearing in many media stories and political speeches which report that social mobility in Britain is getting worse over time (Kelly, 2006). The authors state without caveat that 'intergenerational mobility fell markedly over time in Britain' (p2). They back up this claim by presenting the partial correlations between the incomes of parents and children from two British cohorts. Their Table 5 shows that the income correlation over two generations of the same family was 0.166 for the 1958 National Child Development Study (NCDS) and 0.281 for the 1970 BCS. Therefore, according to these authors, the earlier 1958 British cohort exhibits greater social mobility than the latter. They attribute this change over time to an increase in participation in HE which they claim has benefited middle-class families the most.

Nowhere in the reported findings is it stated that this analysis only applies to male cohort members or that cases without earned income themselves or whose parents were without income were omitted from the analysis. Nowhere in the tables of mobility and transition is it made clear how many cases are missing from the analysis. NCDS 1958 originally had 16,460 cases, of which the Blanden *et al* (2005) study used 2,163 or 13 per cent. BCS 1970 originally had 16,695 cases, of which Blanden *et al* used 1,976 or 12 per cent. This 87 to 88 per cent attrition rate must affect our reliance on the results. We need to ask whether the size of the apparent difference between the two cohorts is large enough to overcome reservations about bias caused by the selection of cases. Given that both cohort studies were sampled differently in the first place, asked different questions in different orders and had the usual levels of measurement error it would be unwise to base policy on there being any genuine underlying difference between the two values. In our judgement, the purported explanations for the difference, such as increasing access to HE, are not needed because the difference in relation to the scale of data problems is not large enough to merit attention.

While such cohort studies are especially prone to attrition, and so to missing cases, exactly the same kind of biases arise with non-response in more traditional 'snapshot' surveys, which have the added disadvantage of not being able to separate out the two dimensions of time. Raffe (2000) uses the Scottish School Leavers Survey to consider the characteristics of 16-19 year-olds who are not in education, employment or training (NEETs). He reports that around 31 per cent of all cases in the survey are NEET at some time in the first three years after the end of compulsory schooling. For most of these young people this inactivity is only a temporary period of transition or adjustment, and Raffe concludes that NEET is a relatively normal state rather than evidence of the existence of a worrying counter-culture feared by some observers. This sounds plausible and may well be correct. However, only around 39 per cent of cases in the relevant cohort responded to the sweep at the start of the period and the sweep at the end. If there were a counter-culture of 'status-zero' youths, rejecting education, employment and training, one might reasonably expect that these individuals would also be less likely to co-operate continuously in a longitudinal study. The 61 per cent of cases missing from the analysis must affect our judgement about the conclusion drawn.

Croxford (2006) provides an excellent summary of some of the major problems faced when conducting an analysis over time using a cohort study, in this case the Youth Cohort Study or YCS. Ironically, these problems include improvements over time in the YCS so that before 1992 it was based on a school clustered sample, whereas from 1992 it is meant to be a simple random sample, to include those who had left school already. This is un-doubtedly an improvement in some ways but means that apparent changes over time could reflect only the changes in sample coverage and quality. It has also led to a higher refusal rate. The survey contractors have changed over time, seeking to cut costs, separating the collection and analysis teams and reducing the input from academics. There have also been numerous changes in the wording of questions which is an almost inevitable occurrence (Gorard, 2001). Like geographical information systems, using cohort studies does not really solve the problems outlined at the start of this chapter; it introduces further complications.

Conclusion

We cannot assess the claims of under-representation in HE using figures from HE alone. We need also to track changes in the social class of the population from which HE entrants come and changes in the distribution of entry quali-fications by social class in that population. These figures have to be combined in appropriate proportions. This takes no account of the inflation taking place in class categories, due partly to the feminisation of the workforce. Non-manual occupations have grown in past decades while both skilled and non-skilled manual occupations have declined, changing the meaning and rela-tive privilege of non-manual occupations. This means that an observation that the proportion of students from non-manual backgrounds has remained the same over a number of years could actually be construed as evidence of wider participation in HE.

This chapter has shown the difficulties an analyst faces even in making an apparently simple comparison between the characteristics of individuals in HE and characteristics of individuals in the population. So the analyst is faced with a judgement about whether there is indeed under-representation of specific social groups, and of whether the proportionate participation of these groups is far enough below one (1) to trigger a search for the cause. The traditional panoply of statistical analyses, such as significance tests, confidence intervals or standard errors cannot help here because these address only the sampling variation due to chance. None of the many analytical decisions and compromises summarised in this chapter concern such sampling variation (Gorard, 2006a). They are much more to do with clarity and good judgement.

The difficulties rehearsed in this chapter often lead analysts to focus mainly on young full-time participants taking their first degree, for whom the data is most complete. The relative quality of data for young full-time participants leads some commentators to take these elements for granted in an uncritical way in their own smaller scale work (e.g. Reay *et al*, 2005). All of this may bias public perception of HE issues, by apparently marginalising part-time and older students. Yet, as we shall argue in the next chapter, these are two groups that the available evidence shows are the most likely to create the widening participation that policy apparently requires.

3

Which students are missing from HE?

Introduction

The UK widening participation agenda is predicated on the notion that particular social groups which are defined by social class or ethnic background are unfairly under-represented in higher education. This situation is now accepted by many policy makers who have introduced schemes to ameliorate it, such as showing preference to candidates from state-funded schools or certain postal code areas (Goddard and Utley, 2004). The situation is even accepted by many researchers who are using case study methods to find out more about the causes. One such is Archer (2000) who justifies her small scale work by stating that participation is lowest among those from unskilled occupational backgrounds: 'the British Higher Education system has undergone a period of considerable growth... yet participation among certain 'non-traditional' social groups remains persistently low' (p2).

However, Chapter Two has already shown how difficult it is to present accurate figures on the under-representation of social groups. Despite these problems, official figures are the best evidence we have. There is not some other, far superior, dataset on which the WP agenda is based. This chapter presents some figures for the HE participation of particular social groups to try to decide which students are 'missing', and so where the efforts of WP activities might be directed. Some of the figures are new, some come from the HEFCE review of evidence (Gorard *et al*, 2006), and some from our other work, especially that for the Rees Reviews of student hardship in Wales (Gorard and Taylor, 2001; Taylor and Gorard, 2005).

Participation overall

There has been a considerable increase in the number of home under-graduate students of all ages in the UK over the past decade, with an overall growth of around 50 per cent (Table 3.1). Much of this increase has been in study for qualifications below degree level (according to HESA), including foundation degrees, diplomas and professional certificates. This distinction is important because it shows that increasing participation and the widening of opportunities that accompanies it has been disproportionately concerned with these relatively recent kinds of opportunities. This means that many of the arguments for HE participation, such as economic ones, based on the traditional first degree model are not applicable (see Chapter Nine).

Table 3.1: Number of home students, UK, 1994/95-2004/05

	1994/95	1999/00	2004/05
All undergraduates	451840	525140	673775
Full-time first degree	273586	281780	320865
Part-time first degree	49425	31400	58285

Source: HESA

Figure 3.1 shows the overall participation rate of Welsh-domiciled 18 to 20 year-olds between 1997/98 and 2002/03. These figures are similar to those for the other home countries of the UK. Recently, increasing participation among traditional-age students has stalled in both England and Wales while the age cohort has grown. One further noteworthy point about these figures is the lack of any clear negative impact on overall participation following the intro-duction of up-front tuition fees in 1998/99. There may have been a slight in-crease in numbers for 1997/98 with students spurning a gap year to avoid paying fees, followed by a slight temporary decline for 1998/99 as these students were already in the system But if successive years are averaged out, there is no sustained impact from the change in funding arrangements on the number of students. This is our first indication of a body of supporting evi-dence, which follows in Chapter Five, to show that finance is not the direct barrier to participation that it might have seemed. Over the same period female participation for 18 to 20 year-olds increased annually between 1997/98 and 2002/03 from 41 per cent to over 43 per cent, perhaps reflecting the increased academic attainment of girls in schools.

Figure 3.1: Participation (percentage of age group) of Welsh-domiciled 18 to 20 year-olds 1997/98 – 2002/03

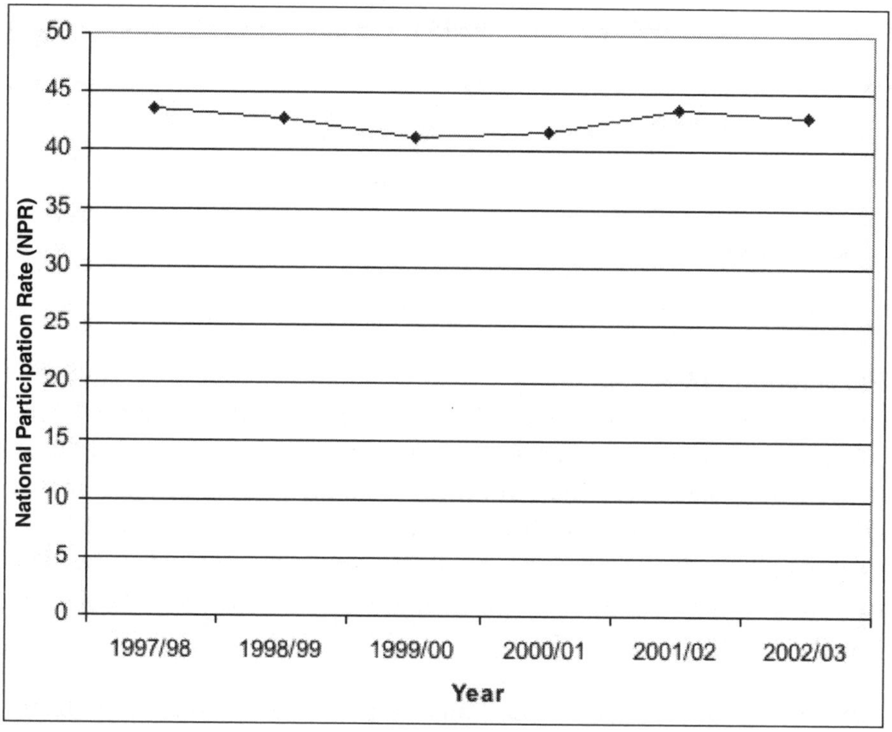

Source: HESA

Participation by age

Table 3.2 shows the age profile of Welsh-domiciled students participating in HE. The proportion of students aged 18 or below increased over this period, mostly representing students aged less than 18, perhaps because the introduction of fees has made deferred entry to HE less attractive. HE is, against expectation, becoming increasingly the preserve of the young, at the expense of those aged 30 or more. Over time one might expect these developments to be related, so that as a higher proportion of the younger cohort take part in HE early so a smaller proportion of the same cohort is available to take part for the first time at a later date. However, the relative increase among younger students is not large enough, in itself, to explain the changes over time. In general, the changes over time in the actual numbers of students are distributed across all age groups.

Table 3.2: Percentage of Welsh-domiciled students by age

	1995/96	2002/03
18 or below	27	35
19	13	12
20	5	5
21-29	19	16
30 or above	38	31

Source: HESA

Participation by social class

Table 3.3 presents a historical breakdown of the student body in the UK by social class according to the Registrar General's previous scale (Gorard, 2003). It shows that students come from predominantly professional and managerial backgrounds (I/II), with few from part-skilled and unskilled backgrounds (IV/V). This pattern changes little over the time period shown. The most consistent change has been in the growth of those students of unknown occupational class.

Table 3.3: Students accepted for home degree in UK 1994/95 to 1998/99

Class	1994	1995	1996	1997	1998
I	16	15	15	14	14
II	41	40	40	39	40
IIIN	12	11	12	12	12
IIIM	16	16	15	14	15
IV	7	7	7	8	8
V	2	2	2	2	2
Not known	8	9	10	11	11

Source: National Statistics (2001)

Table 3.4 shows the proportion of the overall population in each occupational class category also using the Registrar General's previous classification, thus providing an important comparator for figures like those in Table 3.3. These figures show quite clearly that social classes IIIM (skilled manual occupations) to V have been proportionately under-represented in HE, while I to IIIN (non-manual occupations) have been over-represented, although for social class IIIN itself participation in HE is in line with the distribution in the population as a whole. However, it is also important to note that occupational groups are not evenly divided in the population and we would expect there to be many more individuals in HE from class II than from class IV. And this is what we find. The dominance of certain social groups in HE is partly a function of their numerical frequency in the population which changes over historical time, to an extent that is not always made clear in media and policy reports. Another problem is that the population figures are for the economically active head of the household, not for individuals. If the population is becoming more middle-class over time, for example, then we would expect students at HE, who tend to be younger than the population as a whole, to be more middle-class than the resident population. In itself this would not be unfair or even disproportionate in relation to the correct figures for the appropriate age-related population (which we do not have, see Chapter Two).

Table 3.4: Social class of economically active heads of households, Wales, 1991

Occupational class	% All households	% Aged 0-15
I	6	6
II	29	28
IIIN	11	10
IIIM	31	32
IV	15	15
V	5	5
other	3	3
Total	100	100

Source: Census 1991

For traditional-age students, for whom we have superior data, there has been a considerable growth in overall HE participation from 12 per cent of the age cohort in 1980 to 35 per cent in 2001. More dramatically, however, Table 3.5 shows that this growth has been disproportionately among social classes IIIM to V (the under-represented groups), rather than I to IIIN (the over-represented groups). In 1940 an individual in one of the over-represented social classes was four times as likely to go on to HE as one from the under-represented social classes. As recently as 1990 the odds remained at nearly 4:1. But by 2001 an individual from the over-represented social classes was 2.6 times as likely to go to HE, which is still a considerable difference but is at least an improvement. Looked at another way, those in over-represented social classes are now over six times as likely to continue to HE as they were in 1940 whereas the figure for those in under-represented social classes is over nine times. Since 1990, classes I to IIIN have improved their position by a factor of 1.35 (or 50/37) whereas classes IIIM to V have improved theirs by a factor of 1.9 (19/10). Whatever the problem in the current situation is, it is better than it was for young students and in so far as existing figures allow us to judge.

Table 3.5: Age participation index by collapsed social class in UK 1940-2001

Year	I/II/IIIN	IIIM/IV/V	Overall
1940	8	2	-
1950	19	3	-
1960	27	4	-
1970	32	5	-
1980	33	7	12
1985	35	8	14
1990	37	10	19
1991	35	11	23
1992	40	14	28
1993	43	16	30
1994	46	17	32
1995	47	17	32
1996	48	18	33
1997	48	18	34
1998	45	17	32
1999	45	17	32
2000	48	18	33
2001	50	19	35

Note: The API is the number of home-domiciled young (aged less than 21) initial entrants to full-time and sandwich undergraduate courses in higher education expressed as a proportion of the averaged 18 to 19 year-old UK population.

Other commentators and analysts agree on this improvement and its scale (Mayhew *et al*, 2004). Using a different dataset and approach Raffe *et al* (2006) show a long-term decline from 1986 to 1999 in the odds ratios for the managerial/professional class compared to working-class students, in terms of attainment levels at age 16, staying on in formal education at age 16, attainment at 18, and subsequent participation in HE. For these two groups in England, the odds ratios of taking a degree fell from 7.9 in 1990, to 5.7 in 1996, and 4.4 in 1999. The near consensus among these analysts confirms that the

DfES (2003) and authors working in centres sponsored by them (Blanden *et al*, 2005), who claim that the situation is actually getting worse in terms of social class participation, are simply wrong (see Chapter Five). In fact, HE participation has been slowly widening for decades.

The fastest growth in widening participation between the two collapsed social class groups in Table 3.5 occurred in a short period of the early 1990s, reflecting little more than a rapid increase in the number of places available at HE institutions (Figure 3.2). However, there has also been a more general increase over time as part of a relatively long-term historical and social trend. This trend is usually undisturbed by specific policies to widen participation, including those in current vogue which are actually associated with the end of the long-term improvement. This suggests that the quickest and easiest and possibly even the cheapest way to widen participation is simply to increase the number of funded places at HEIs. The HEIs will find the students if there are places to be filled, and the historical evidence is that these new students will be disproportionately from the under-represented social groups.

Figure 3.2: Changes in odds ratios of participation in HE, social classes 1990-2001

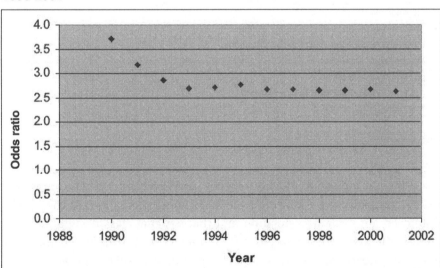

Table 3.6 shows the socio-economic composition of Welsh-domiciled students participating in HE in 2002/03. There are serious limitations in any analysis of this kind. The socio-economic classifications derived from UCAS admission data ignore the 38 per cent of all Welsh-domiciled students who

did not enter HE through UCAS and a further 28 per cent of UCAS-entered students were not classifiable. This means that socio-economic classifications are only available for 34 per cent of students and even these will contain both errors and areas of subjective judgement. Presenting the table in this way, making the missing cases visible in both columns, is unorthodox and somewhat inconvenient for readers. But it should be effective in alerting readers to the scale of the problem. There is no alternative higher quality or more complete dataset on which the WP agenda can be based. The data presented here are the best available. What they show above all is that no one really knows the socio-economic make-up of the population or of HE students in enough detail to make clear claims about the proportional differences between small groups or relatively minor changes over time.

Table 3.6: Percentage of Welsh-domiciled students participating in HE by socio-economic classification 2002/03 compared with population census 2001

	HE 2002/03	Population census 2001
Higher managerial and professional occupations	6	6
Lower managerial and professional occupations	11	16
Intermediate occupations	5	8
Small employers and own account workers	3	7
Lower supervisory and technical occupations	2	8
Semi-routine occupations	4	12
Routine occupations	2	10
Never worked and long-term unemployed	0	4
Not classified or not valid	67	29

Source: HESA

There is some indication that both higher- and lower-managerial and professional occupational backgrounds are over-represented amongst the Welsh-domiciled HE student population and that working-class occupations, including the long-term unemployed, routine and semi-routine occupations and lower supervisory and technical occupations are under-represented. The picture for only those students aged 18-30 is similar (Taylor and Gorard, 2005). However, it must be considered, given that a majority of the data is missing, that the difference may lie not only in the student population but also who answers the question about occupational background. If, for example, higher managerial and professional occupations were proportiona-tely represented in HE but more likely to respond to the occupational ques-tion, the result would be indistinguishable from what we see here. As with the problem of historical changes in the class structure of the relevant popula-tion, we simply do not know about the impact of differential response rates. This means, of course, that we do not really know whether and to what extent different social classes are under-represented in HE and this problem does not only apply to social class.

Participation by ethnic groups

Although the chief focus of the WP agenda is on occupational background, it is worth briefly considering the situation in relation to ethnic background. Many of the same issues of comparison and data quality apply. Although there has been a steady improvement in the completeness of the figures for ethnicity to over 90 per cent (Table 3.7), the ISRs of those in HE show a con-siderable number of students of unknown ethnic origin. In addition, the ethnic classifications used by HESA have changed over time and in Wales especially the proportion of any other group than white is so small that the percentages are extremely volatile. Therefore, missing data means that it is not possible to detect any robust trends for specific minority backgrounds.

Table 3.7: Percentage of students with known ethnicity UK 1994/95-2004/05

	1994/95	1999/00	2004/05
All undergraduates	80	90	91
Full-time first degree	83	94	97
Part-time first degree	80	87	87
Source: HESA			

Table 3.8: Percentage of white students UK 1994/95-2004/05

	1994/95	1999/00	2004/05
All undergraduates	87	87	84
Full-time first degree	87	84	81
Part-time first degree	90	88	87
Source: HESA			

The proportion of students with known ethnicity who are non-white has increased slightly over a decade in the UK (Table 3.8). This increase is approximately in line with, but slightly ahead of, an overall increase in ethnic minorities in the population as a whole.

In Wales, the proportion of students where ethnicity is declared not known has declined since 1995, perhaps because the use of more precise ethnic classifications has encouraged greater response rates (Table 3.9). Therefore, the increase in the number of students from other ethnic groups, including white, is largely a result of better recording and reporting of this data. But there continue to be many more students who refuse to provide this information than the number of students who report that they are non-white.

Table 3.9: Percentage of Welsh-domiciled students in HE by ethnic origin

	1995/96	2002/03
White (all)	82	85
Not known or refused	17	11
Other ethnicity	2	4
Source: HESA		

The proportion of home students domiciled in Wales from ethnic minority backgrounds is between 3 per cent and 4 per cent and increasing (3.1% in 1998 (UCAS, 2000), 3.3% in 1999 and 3.7% in 2000 (HESA Higher Education Management Statistics). According to the quarterly Labour Force Survey the population of Wales aged 18-30 contains about 2 per cent from ethnic minority backgrounds. In the 1991 census 2.2 per cent of the population of Wales aged 10-14 was classified as non-white. It could be argued that the HE system slightly over-represents these groups, if we assume that all ethnic groups are equally likely to answer the question about ethnic background. But this does not take into account the fact that ethnic minority students generally obtain higher qualifications than white students at NQF levels 2 and 3, making them differentially eligible for HE acceptance. Nor does it take into account potential inequalities between subjects, institutions, regions, and specific backgrounds. We can say that existing figures give us no reason to assume that ethnic minorities, in general, are under-represented in the HE systems of England or Wales.

Participation by sex

Since 1994/95, the proportion of female first degree students in HE has grown considerably, especially among part-time students in the UK (Table 3.10). In Wales 54 per cent of all Welsh-domiciled students in HE were female in 1995/96, rising to 58 per cent by 2002/03. The participation gap between women and men is increasing in all home countries of the UK.

Table 3.10: Percentage of female students UK 1994/95-2004/05

	1994/95	1999/00	2004/05
Full-time first degree	49	53	53
Part-time first degree	53	65	65
Source: HESA			

Part of the explanation may lie in demographics. There are simply more women than men in the population. Another part lies in the purported under-achievement of boys at school (Gorard *et al*, 2001a), and part may be due to positive attitudes towards continuing education among young women, especially at age 16. The participation gap is clear, because there are fewer missing cases in answer to questions about sex/gender than about occupation or ethnicity. It is robust in the sense that it appears annually and is growing. Ironically, this is one area where WP is not particularly active, reflecting a lack of policy concern with the under-representation of males.

Participation by disability

In the UK there has been an increase in the proportion of HE students reporting a disability. In fact the proportion has almost doubled over a decade (Table 3.11).

Table 3.11: Percentage of students with disability UK 1994/95-2004/05

	1994/95	1999/00	2004/05
All undergraduates	3	4	6
Full-time first degree	4	5	7
Part-time first degree	3	3	5
Source: HESA			

It is not clear whether this increase in students with a reported disability is evidence of a widening of opportunities or to do with an increase in reporting. However, it is clear that the major part of the increase is in students with a non-visible disability such as dyslexia (Table 3.12). If the figures for dyslexia are subtracted from the figures for disability, there has been no overall growth in the proportion of disabled students since 1994/95.

Table 3.12: Percentage of students with dyslexia UK 1994/95-2004/05

	1994/95	1999/00	2004/05
All undergraduates	0	1	3
Full-time first degree	1	2	4
Part-time first degree	0	1	1

Source: HESA

Similarly, the number of Welsh-domiciled students participating in HE who report that they have some form of disability increased between 1995/96 and 2002/03. And for many forms of disability this rise has kept pace with the overall increase in Welsh-domiciled students participating in HE (Table 3.13). The main exception to this has been the proportion of students who report they are dyslexic (an increase from 0.5% of all students in 1995/96 to 1.9% of all students in 2002/03).

Table 3.13: Percentage of Welsh-domiciled students in HE with disabilities

Nature of disability	1995/96	2002/03
No known disability	91	92
Not known or not sought	5	2
Dyslexia	1	2
Blind/are partially sighted	0	0
Deaf/have a hearing impairment	0	0
Wheelchair user/have mobility difficulties	1	0
Personal care support	0	0
Mental health difficulties	0	0
An unseen disability	2	1
Multiple disabilities	0	1
Other disability, not listed	1	1

Source: HESA

Note: cell values are rounded to the nearest integer, and so zero represents a value smaller than 0.5 per cent.

Participation by mode of study

Around half of the Welsh-domiciled students in HE are enrolled on full-time courses (Table 3.14), and this proportion changes little over the years. Most of the remainder are part-time students. The classification 'other' students largely consists of those not actively following a programme of study at any-time during that year. This figure has increased since the introduction of tuition fees in 1998/89, which may reflect increased quality of reporting or this may be some evidence of a deterrent effect of fees (see Chapter Five).

Table 3.14: Percentage of each mode of study for Welsh-domiciled students in HE

Mode of study	1995/96	2002/03
Full-time	50	52
Part-time	43	42
Sandwich course	7	4
Other	0	3

Source: HESA

Participation by area of residence

The Participation Rate Ratio (see HEFCW, 2000; Shuttleworth *et al*, 2001; Gorard and Taylor, 2001) is the ratio of the number of students who actually attend HE from a given area of residence, to the relevant total population of that area, multiplied by the national participation rate. In other words, the PRR compares the participation rate of a particular area to the national level of participation, while standardising for the unequal distribution of the population across the country. For convenience of analysis, the figures discussed in this section are for 18 to 20 year-olds in HE and in the population (see Chapter Two). Examining these ratios over time and place reveals an interesting and robust pattern (Gorard and Taylor, 2001; Taylor and Gorard, 2005; HEFCE, 2005).

In 1995/96, 16 per cent of 18-20 year olds living in the least 'income deprived' wards in Wales entered HE. Areas of relative affluence, such as Monmouth-shire, have the highest participation rate ratios, well above the national parti-cipation rates. But they have the slowest increase in PRRs over time, from 155 in 1995/96 to 193 in 2002/03. This compares quite dramatically with only 5 per cent of 18-20 year olds living in the most 'income deprived' wards who attended HE in 1995/96 (Gorard and Taylor, 2001). Areas of relative poverty such as Blaenau Gwent have low PRRs. But they have the highest relative increase in PRRs from 51 in 1995/96 to 72 in 2002/03. Although large differences in the rates of participation remain, these trends mean that the rates of participation of 18 to 20 year olds across Wales are homogenising. This process of homogenisation from 1995/96 to 2002/03 occurred irrespective of the policies in force, such as tuition fees, perhaps as part of a longer-term trend in the homogenisation of prior attainment (Gorard, 2000). These figures therefore confirm the analysis by social class already described that HE is generally becoming more equitable over time.

The relevance of prior qualifications

The overwhelming majority of applicants to university are accepted on the basis of their prior qualifications (around 95% according to UCAS 1999), and two-thirds are accepted on the basis of A/AS levels alone. The first thing to notice about the relationship between these prior qualifications is their very strong association with social class. According to the Youth Cohort Study (YCS), 51 per cent of social classes I/II in England obtained the equivalent of two A-levels at age 18-19 in 1993. According to the National Audit Office around 56 per cent of the same group obtained NQF level 3 or its equivalent. On the other hand, the figures are 28 per cent for social classes IIIM/IV/V, 8 per cent for classes IV/V and 13 per cent for class V (YCS in 1993). This means that we should expect HE places, awarded competitively in terms of prior qualification, to be taken disproportionately by those from the higher social classes. Given that social class I is only one fifth of the size of social class II, their combined weighted average age participation index (API) for 1995 is 53 per cent, or 50 per cent for Wales in 2000 (Table 3.15). This is almost exactly the same as the proportion of each social class attaining level 3 qualifications for entry to HE. This means that social classes I/II were represented in HE entirely proportionately to their prior qualifications. The participation rate for social class V in 1995 is 12 per cent, again in line with or even above their qualification rate according to the National Audit Office or YCS.

Table 3.15: Age participation rate in Wales and UK by collapsed social class 2000

	Wales	UK
I/II	50	53
IIIN/M	27	30
IV/V	14	8
Source: Callender and Kemp (2001)		

In 1989, the proportion of suitably qualified 18-19 year-olds who attended HE was 65 per cent. By 1992 that had risen to 90 per cent and is now higher still. A recent report by the House of Commons Select Committee on Education and Skills suggested a qualified age participation rate of 97 per cent. This is what the analysis above confirms. 'Lower academic attainment at age 18 accounts for most of the lower participation in higher education by 18 year olds from poorer social classes' (National Audit Office, 2002, p11). This summary is in line with that of the DfES (2003), which points out that 18 per cent of people from manual or unskilled backgrounds gain two A-levels by the age of 18 and that this proportion is exactly the same as the proportion in HE. Therefore, the qualified age participation index is at or near 100 per cent, although this official statistic is no longer calculated. At the higher end of attainment, for those gaining 25+ UCAS points (the old tariff system), 97 per cent from higher social classes and 94 per cent from lower go on to HE. Of those with 13-24 UCAS points the figures for participation are 92 per cent and 88 per cent (Connor and Dewson, 2001). This means that we can explain the stratification in young peoples' participation in HE almost entirely by the stratification of their prior qualifications. To establish that groups are unfairly represented in HE we must show either that these prior qualifications are unfairly distributed or that it is unfair to use prior qualifications as a basis for access to HE.

Conclusions

Chapters Two and Three have established how difficult it is to decide which social groups are under-represented in HE in the UK and by how much. The best available datasets suggest that there is no simple and consistent pattern of under-representation among socially disadvantaged groups in HE, once prior qualifications for entry are taken into account (see also Chapter Six). Under-representation is already in evidence in terms of the possession of entry qualifications at NQF level 3 and these are based almost entirely on staying-on rates in schools and colleges, which are based almost entirely on NQF level 2 qualifications, and so on (Gorard and Smith, 2004). This suggests that WP activities need to be directed at the earlier life of potential students rather than at the point of possible transfer to HE. In Chapter Four, we assess the nature and quality of the evidence on overcoming the barriers to WP and from Chapter Five onwards we summarise the best of the available evidence in life-long order.

4

Reviewing the evidence base on widening participation

Introduction

A s explained in Chapter One, we begin our summary of the existing evidence (other than the simple numeric data dealt with in Chapter Three) with a consideration of the kinds of material sought for inclusion in the review and a commentary on the range and quality of the material found. Our approach in the rest of this book is to take a life-long view of the decision to participate in HE. Therefore, evidence relating to early life factors that influence participation, such as family, peer-group and initial education, is crucial. These factors all help to build the learning trajectory of individuals that leads them to consider HE as a possibility. Also relevant is evidence relating to their course and institution selection, barriers within HE, retention, the policy and structure of HE in England, the allocation of places, the funding arrangements, the geography of opportunities, entry requirements, the labour market, the structural barriers to access and retention and the practices and policies of widening participation of currently under-represented groups undertaken nationally, regionally, by sector or institutions, including the success of initiatives to overcome the structural barriers to access. Taken as a whole this list is potentially very wide and could cover almost any societal or life experience so the emphasis here is on those factors which have a plausible direct influence on later participation in HE. Nevertheless, our account tries to be reasonably representative of the wider social, contextual and early schooling literature and of the more specific recent WP literature in England and the other home countries of the UK.

We consider two different elements of change over time. In the first, we ask over historical time between successive cohorts as equality legislation and WP funds come into play, what has been the impact on participation? Who gets what, and what are the remaining obstacles? We began to address these issues in Chapters Two and Three. For the second element of change over the life course of the individual within one cohort, we ask: when do barriers, differences, and problems emerge? What can we do about these in the longer term? In the short term, what can we do to compensate for these differences? Our tentative answers to these questions appear in Chapters Five to Nine. This chapter explains our approach to synthesising the evidence we found in the literature and exemplifies some of the generic problems we encountered.

Searching for the evidence

As part of the collation of evidence relevant to widening participation in higher education we advertised for evidence, proactively contacted key email lists and organisations, and systematically searched journals and websites. As with any other review (Kahn and Macdonald, 2004), the search also involved bibliographies, electronic databases, and hand-searching of key documents. We also added literature known to us from our previous work in the field.

We tried to be as inclusive as possible, searching for and identifying a wide range of published and informal literature. Evidence can be in any form, of any scale, using any method. Material encountered during the search was rejected on only two grounds. These were lack of relevance to the review and not being research related. The contemporary access and widening participation agenda in the UK can be traced back to 1997, specifically to the report of the National Committee of Inquiry into Higher Education, chaired by Lord Dearing (Dearing, 1997), which coincided with the election of a New Labour administration. We focused largely on literature published from this date onward.

Our synthesis has a primary focus on current and future undergraduate education in England. Higher Education is interpreted as Level Four provision or above in any institution, whether designated HE or FE, including foundation degrees and postgraduate progression. However, evidence from other places, such as other home countries of the UK and other sectors of education are included where it is especially powerful or relevant. Our critical appraisal of each study that we have judged to be both relevant and research-related consists of three further judgements: the quality of the research reporting, the nature of the evidence and the quality of the evidence. The remainder of this chapter presents a discussion of these three issues, using extended examples as illustrations.

Quality of research and reporting

Judgement of the usefulness of evidence depends heavily on the quality of reporting. We should expect research to contain somewhere within its report all of the basic information needed for another researcher to replicate the work, including the analysis. If relevant, we may need to know the number of cases, how they were selected, the research design, instruments, context of data collection, methods of analysis and prevalence of findings. These should conventionally be summarised at the start of the report. We should also expect a description of what has been found, including a description of the evidence and not merely an account of what the researchers believe this evidence to mean. These minimum criteria are not especially demanding, yet many of the reports reviewed for this book do not contain this information. The situation has not changed much in education research since similar complaints were made by Tooley with Darby (1998).

Reports differed considerably in the amount of information they gave about the nature and methods of research. Reports giving more information of this type cannot be automatically favoured over others that do not, given that the information provided may show up flaws in the research. But reports that did not give full information (and so do not allow the showing up of flaws) must not be favoured over fuller reports. In the absence of any research methods information the reviewer must assume the worst. Where totally insufficient information was given in a report then we have generally excluded it from further consideration, as though it were the equivalent of a non-research report. Therefore our review of evidence relies almost exclusively on the best reported research. The quality of reporting is high enough in these cases to start a discussion of the fit between research questions, methods, evidence and the conclusions drawn. However, even in this best reported category of research there are numerous problems for a reviewer.

One of our first findings is that a substantial proportion of ostensible research reports did not actually report new research evidence or analysis of any kind. This phenomenon has been noted before in other contexts (Gorard *et al*, 2004a). There were literature reviews which are useful for future reviewers as a ready source of references and, if they have been conducted rigorously and sceptically, can provide a useful synthesis of an entire area. There were also some research method and methodological pieces which were thought-provoking and helpful. But in addition to these, the research literature contained a high proportion of thought-pieces with no clear empirical content, no summary of the research of others and no assistance to others intending to conduct research. We generally excluded these three categories from further consideration.

Having eliminated many of these thought pieces and all reports with insufficient description of methods or findings, we focused on the remainder which were reasonably well-described empirical studies. Of these, a high pro-portion showed substantial defects. Research reports, especially of work traditionally termed qualitative, regularly presented their conclusions as though these were the findings and presented the actual evidence for the conclusions sparsely often as illustrations. In such reports there is no way of knowing how widespread any finding is or how likely it is that a different analyst would reach similar conclusions. Only the illustrations actually pro-vided in the reports can be used safely as the evidence in a review. This is not always so and higher quality reports describe the prevalence of patterns more clearly or present some form of validation of the analysis (Ball *et al*, 2002). Research reports of complex statistical models produced the same sort of problems for a reviewer, where the reviewer does not have access to the data-set and the actual data is not summarised clearly.

Other than weaknesses in reporting the evidence, the most common generic defect was the link between the evidence presented and the conclusions drawn from it. There were a number of repeated problems, some of them out-side the control of the researchers themselves. These included deficient data-sets, lack of controlled interventions, lack of suitable comparators, routine exclusion of those not participating in education and lack of agreement about how to compare differences over time and place (see also Chapter Two). A typical piece of work in this field involved a small number of interviews with a group of existing participants in education, often from the same institution as the researcher. Such a study cannot uncover a causal model, is difficult to generalise from and tells us nothing about non-participants which is the group with whom much work in this field is ostensibly concerned. These flaws are so common and not specific to research about widening participa-tion in education that they are not generally remarked on by authors, picked up in peer review, or taken into account when attempting to draw warranted conclusions from one or more studies.

The general pattern of research problems encountered during our review is not about the quality or desirability of different methods of investigation or analysis nor about whether the conclusions drawn by researchers could be shown to be true by other means. The common problem is that the research reports do not provide the evidence to support their conclusions. The conclusions are not warranted by the evidence presented to support them (Gorard, 2002a). This complaint applies even more strongly to reports that present conclusions based on poorly reported research. This does not mean that the evidence presented is not in some way valid, so we did not exclude a research report from our review because its authors reach erroneous conclusions. We largely ignored the background, theory and conclusions of research reports anyway, and focused on the description of the methods and the findings as directly reported. This approach allows a larger number of pieces to be involved than in a traditional synthesis but allots some of them a much smaller role than others.

Traditionally the validity of research has been assessed partly in terms of whether it has been evaluated or peer reviewed (Kahn and Macdonald, 2004). Peer review is the major quality control mechanism for academic publications, but is inconsistent between publishers, journals and reviewers. It also tends to suppress innovative and imaginative work, can create a 'file-drawer' problem so that only 'significant' results are published and can take so long that it leads to the publication of already dated work. On this basis, it was decided that it is not possible to rely on any kind of kitemark for the quality of evidence. It is not the case that passing peer review to appear in a prestigious journal is in itself a guarantee of quality in research or research reporting. Nor is it possible to rely on work from specific individuals, institutions or organisations.

Some studies had several reports based on the same dataset, perhaps intended for different audiences. It is vital for any weighting process that the same evidence is not used twice. Therefore we used the best complete report of the methods and findings and in this case omitted alternative versions from further consideration. Some reports have evidence from more than one study or dataset. This is not a problem for the approach which we adopted where we focused on the findings themselves rather than any form of vote-counting of the conclusions.

Some generic problems of research

The remainder of this chapter illustrates through examples representing a more general picture why we are not able to use the source, author, method, or scale of research reports as any guarantee of quality. It also demonstrates our claim that the major problem lies in the conclusions drawn by the reports' authors.

Rigorous experimental approaches to the widening of participation in HE are rare. For example, in a review of literature Hudson (2005a) reported many examples of creative WP activities but no rigorous evaluation of the impact of these activities. In fact there were no evaluations of any kind. In our review we encountered no evidence based even loosely on an experimental design. In the absence of clear evidence about what works to widen participation it is difficult to justify using public money for any unwarranted intervention, policy or practice. In the situation where a controlled experimental intervention to detect a cause effect relationship is not possible (Gorard, 2002b), it is still possible to compare research findings for the area or group in focus with the equivalent findings for another group. This must be done carefully but is not technically difficult. Presumably it is rare in the widening participation literature partly because it involves more research and so greater expense. If we look at the impact of the introduction of tuition fees on patterns of participation, we need to consider the patterns both before and after the introduction of fees and to look at both those who do and do not participate. Instead of these four data readings which are essential to make even tentative claims about impact, a typical study would involve only a consideration of current participants often in the institution of the researcher. This convenient approach to gathering evidence is unfortunately widespread.

For example, an evaluation of Aimhigher, originally Excellence Challenge, intended to improve access to HE for young students from poor backgrounds, was actually a report of the WP activities undertaken by HEIs (Pennell *et al*, 2004). It contained self-reports from HEIs of increased applications from specific groups but no proportionate analysis. In seven chapters reporting research on the impact of Foundation Degrees, Beaney (2006) reports no attempt to look at their impact on patterns of participation.

A series of booklets entitled 'Making a difference: the impact of Aimhigher' have been published showing no evidence at all of impact on patterns of participation. In Action on Access (2005a), despite the impact suggested by the title and a section in each case study entitled 'how the activity made a difference', the results are not clear. It contains general and unsustained comments such as 'feedback from the conference was very positive and comments included...' (p32) or 'It has opened up many eyes and been a positive learning curve' (p30) or 'information and advice... was given to twelve women... and at least four made serious enquiries about higher education' (p17). There is no comparison group and so no counterfactual. In this example, not only does the reader not know exactly how many of the twelve women enquired about HE, they also do not know whether any of them applied, or how many of them would have been interested without the intervention. On page 18 the report describes a questionnaire and how many people it was distributed to but says nothing about how many were returned or what the results were. Action on Access (2005b) is similar, with comments such as 'Mentees [those mentored] have expressed high levels of satisfaction with the scheme' (p15). Action on Access (2005c) points out that

> at this stage in the programme, it is not possible to provide hard evidence about the impact upon progression to HE but there is evidence that the printed materials have been well received by providers. (p29)

Action on Access (2005d) claims success because: 'positive and proactive engagement with a hard-to-reach group has led all partners to challenge their perceptions of one another' (p20) and even claims success because 'the HE students [acting for the intervention] gain a range of benefits including the opportunity to earn a little money' (p17). According to these reports, all interventions have been uniformly successful but there is no evidence that a single individual has attended HE as a result. These pieces are typical reports of work in this field.

Missing comparators

In the absence of trials and with studies often lacking suitable comparators or time series, it is difficult to show a causal connection. A simple example of reporting unwarranted causation, unwarranted because of no comparison over time or between groups, comes from the Sutton Trust (2004, p5):

> Since 1997, universities, the Government and the Sutton Trust have been funding a range of programmes – such as summer schools, partnerships between schools and universities, and the use of outreach officers – to make it easier for suitably qualified state school students to apply to our leading universities. Again, the facts about the impact of these initiatives should be allowed to speak for themselves: both the number and the proportion of state school students entering these institutions has increased considerably over 5 years.

This claim manages to combine ignorance of the need for a comparison or control group with the problems of uncontrolled multiple interventions and the fallacy that temporal association is the same as causation (Gorard, 2002b). The Sutton Trust authors can have no idea whether any of these interventions were effective and which were not or whether the same changes in university applications would have occurred in the absence of any of them. For example, Gorard (2000) shows that the A-level results of students from state-funded schools have been catching up with those from private schools as part of a trend that is more widespread than the impact of the initiatives described by the Sutton Trust and which pre-date 1997. The results for private schools in England were nearer reaching a threshold effect in 1997 than the results for state schools. In an era of annual improvement in A-level scores we would expect an increased proportion of applications and acceptances at HE for state-funded students even in the absence of any intervention at all. The more useful questions are not whether or not state schools' applications increased since the inception of this range of programmes but whether they have increased by substantially more than would be predicted by longer historical trends and whether they have done so specifically in the geographical areas and sectors most affected by the programmes. We have no idea.

This example illustrates two important lessons for this book. The criticism of the implied causal conclusions drawn by the Sutton Trust (2004) does nothing to disturb their evidence. The evidence shows that the number and proportion of state school entrants to good universities has risen. This is not necessarily in dispute. What is disputed is the warrant that leads to the causal conclusion (Gorard, 2002a). Therefore, in a critical appraisal of evidence on WP, the evidence of such a study should be included, while the conclusions are discarded. The evidence in the Sutton Trust report is presented clearly enough for this separation of findings and conclusions to be made. In many pieces the conclusions are presented at the expense of the evidence or with only indications of what the evidence might be. We cannot privilege such reports over those like the Sutton Trust that give us enough information to see whether the conclusions are not entailed by the data.

Missing comparators are widespread in the studies we reviewed. UCAS applicant figures give us no idea at all about who is not applying to university and yet numerous analyses are reported without making the implications of this deficit clear. The Rees Report (2001) on student hardship in Wales asked students whether lack of finance was a hindrance to their participation. It did not ask individuals who were not students whether lack of finance was a barrier to their participation. This would take longer and involve a harder to identify and reach sub-sample of the population that may have been influenced by changes in student finance.

A rather extreme version of the lack of comparator comes from Lawy (2000), even though this concerns a non-participant. This paper illustrates the experience of one person who left formal education at the age of 16 and started work. The main finding is that this person continued to learn even outside formal education. We have no way of knowing from this evidence whether people who stay in education or who leave education but do not start work also continue to learn. Our guess is that most do. The fact that one school leaver continues to learn when they start work does not, for us, change the truth status of any prior proposition. As such, the evidence is of no research consequence but still appears as a peer reviewed paper in a high status research journal.

A more substantial piece of work that also illustrates a missing comparator problem was funded by the DfES. 'Action Learning in the Community' was a large action research project conducted in two universities and four other sites including adult education and community colleges (Learning from Experience Trust, 2003, mimeo). The research explored 'innovative ways of attracting and retaining potential students from some of the most socially excluded and marginalised groups in society' (p1). The summary report describes the various actions undertaken in support of this key aim but does not describe whether they made any difference. As the report states 'we have no longitudinal data on ultimate success of the student cohort or their ultimate levels of retention or success' (p6). If the project was too brief to allow follow-up data to be analysed then it was a waste of money as research and there is no way of knowing whether it was also a waste of money as action.

Another strand of this same general problem is represented by the work of Archer (2002), on the post-16 educational choice of Muslim girls. The article does not establish whether there is a particular problem with the post-16 participation of Muslim girls that is worth researching. Other studies suggest that women of Pakistani and Bangladeshi origin, among whom we would expect to find many census Muslims, are well qualified and well represented in post-compulsory education (e.g. Ahmad, 2001). The research discusses with 14-16 year-old students whether longer term societal changes have made it easier for Muslim women in north west England to participate post-16 and quotes their responses as evidence. But it is debatable whether 14- to 16-year-olds are the best source of information on past changes in post-16 educational opportunities and what emphasis we should give to their opinions on what their choices might have been like three, five or ten years ago. These students are not necessarily wrong. They may, for example, be correctly portraying the knowledge of others, but the conclusions of the researcher cannot be based securely on this evidence.

Although the comments of some Muslim boys are presented in the paper, none of the comments are presented with their relative prevalence among the (unknown) number of boys and girls in the study. It is also interesting how few individuals are quoted even though a few are quoted repeatedly. Therefore, there is no reason to believe that the comments from girls could not equally have come from boys and vice versa. Because there is no non-Muslim group we have no way of knowing whether the same comments could equally well have been made by non-Muslims. When a student describes how Muslim girls have more freedom than in the old days (p370) we do not know whether this increase in freedom is true or illusory nor whether it would also feature in the stories of non-Muslim girls. Similarly, when Muslims suggest that their parents are influential in their decision to participate in post-16 education this suggests think that these comments are specific to this group. Biggart *et al* (2004) suggest from a much larger-scale study that parents are the major influence for 16 year-olds in all social groups.

A large number of the studies we encountered similarly did not have groups against which the findings could be compared. Barrett's (1999) study described twelve white males who were not expected to achieve benchmark GCSE qualifications, deciding whether or not to remain in education post-16. The majority of these students wanted to continue in post-compulsory education but their reasons for following particular routes in particular colleges were not compared with students who were likely to achieve higher scores in school examinations. This absence of a comparison group means that we do not know whether the views of the sample were typical of the students in the study or whether students of higher ability would view the barriers to study and the choice process any differently. This limits the applicability of the results and questions any use that researchers and education providers can make of the findings.

Inappropriate comparators

Even when explicit comparisons are made in research reports, they are too frequently inappropriate. In one influential study for HE (see Chapter Two), Blanden *et al* (2005) claim that inter-generational income mobility is much less in Britain than in six other comparator states:

> International comparisons indicate that intergenerational mobility in Britain is of the same order of magnitude as in the US, but that these countries are substantially less mobile than Canada and the Nordic countries. (p2)

Their Table 2 shows that the income correlation over two generations was 0.271 for Britain (1970, BCS) but only 0.139 for Norway. Therefore social mobility is reportedly lower in Britain than in Norway and the other Scandinavian countries, Canada and West Germany. The researchers are ready with reasons to explain the poor social mobility in Britain, largely on the basis that it has declined with increased access to HE over the decades, an increase that has largely favoured the middle-classes.

Their international comparison uses cohorts from 1958 in Norway, from 1958-1960 in Denmark and Finland and from 1962 in Sweden (see Table 4.1 repeated from p6 of their paper). The authors then compare the results from the 1970 British cohort with the 1958 Norway cohort and others to reach their conclusion that social mobility is worse in Britain than elsewhere. The paper contains no account of why this unlikely comparison, in terms of historical periods, is preferred. If the income correlation over generations from the 1958 British cohort (quoted by the authors in another context as 0.166 in their own Table 5, and see Chapter Two) is compared to the other four countries in Table 4.1, then the conclusion would be that (male) social mobility is about the same in Britain and in Scandinavia and less than in the US, Canada and West Germany.

Table 4.1: Internationally comparable estimates of intergenerational mobility

Country	Sons born (year)	Partial correlation
Britain	1970	.271
Norway	1958	.139
Denmark	1958-1960	.143
Sweden	1962	.143
Finland	1958-1960	.147

Source: Blanden et al *(2005)*

These problems have been pointed out to the authors of the report because of the dangers which stem from its high visibility. However, Blanden *et al* (2006) still claim to have found a drop in income mobility between 1958 and 1970 but no longer use their own analysis to claim that mobility in the UK is low compared with international peers. Instead they make the same point but now reference the work of Jantti *et al* (2006), saying that (p2) 'the level of mobility in the UK is low by international standards (Jantii [sic] *et al*, 2006)'. In fact, Jantti *et al* said nothing of the sort. They used the 1958 figures for Britain as the best comparator and found that the partial correlations for the UK are much closer to Finland, Sweden and Norway than to the US. They conclude: 'The United Kingdom bears a closer resemblance to the Nordic countries than to the United States' (p5) and this finding is even reflected in the title of their paper. Blanden *et al* (2006) are just plain wrong.

The DfES (2003) states that the gap in achievement between social groups starts early and that 'the attainment gap continues to widen through the phases of education, although the pace of increase slows down once children reach 7 years of age'. But such comparisons are not possible. There is no standard test that can be given to students of all ages to test for gaps in attainment. What this statement really means is that the arbitrary percentages of students attaining a series of different threshold scores at each age get larger with age. It treats the expected level of 2 at Key Stage 1 and level 4 at Key Stage 2, or the percentage able to read and write at age 6 with the percentage gaining five or more GCSEs at age 16, as though they were based on the same metric. But given that the expected level is arbitrary, not cross-moderated and not calibrated against the cohort to which it applies, we can change the size of the apparent achievement gap between social groups simply by changing the expected levels. Again the comparisons are inappropriate.

Work presenting numeric analyses also routinely presents differences between groups over time or place without regard to the scale of the numbers in which the differences appear. As an extreme illustration, imagine a social system with only two hypothetical social classes (A and B), in which 1 per cent of social class A attend HE while none of social class B do. In this society all HE students come from class A, and to be born to class B means no chance at all of education at university. Now imagine a similar society with the same two classes, in which 50 per cent of social class A and 49 per cent of social class B attend HE. Would it be true to say that equity between social classes is the same in both societies? Clearly not. But according to the government, most of the media and many academics, both these societies are precisely equal in their equity of access to HE by social class. Their logic would be that the difference between the participation rates in the first society is 1 per cent (1-0) and in the second society it is also 1 per cent (50-49). This misunderstanding of the use of numbers when comparing changes over time or place between two or more groups is widespread (Gorard, 2000).

This kind of error appears in the DfES (2003) report *Widening participation in higher education*. On page 7, the report presents a graph showing the participation rates in HE from 1960 to 2000 of two social groups: those created by collapsing the genuine social classes I, II and IIIN, and classes IIIM, IV, and V. In the year 2000, 48 per cent of the first group (non-manual) and 18 per cent of the second group (manual) attended HE as full-time traditional age students. In 1990, the figures had been around 37 per cent and 10 per cent respectively (Table 4.2) and the DfES describe this earlier position as better in terms of equality of access because 37 minus 10 is less than 48 minus 18. They even claim that 'if one turned the clock back to 1960 when there were just 200,000 full-time students, the gap between the two groups was actually less than it is now'. This claim is based on the simplistic sum that 27 minus 4 is less than 48 minus 18. Presumably if the 1950 figures had been 22 per cent and 0 per cent, with no one at all attending HE from the less privileged group, then the DfES would describe this as better still in terms of equity because 22-0 is even lower than 27-4.

Table 4.2: Participation rates by social class over time

Social class	1960	1990	2000
I/II/IIIN	27	37	48
IIIM/IV/V	4	10	18

What the DfES have done is to use a difference between two numbers with no regard to the size of the numbers involved as though an increase of ten miles per hour for a bicycle was the same as for a jet aircraft. Viewed proportionately the situation in 2000 is actually more equal than in 1990 which is more equal than in 1960. A person in the manual group had around four and a half times as much chance of attending HE in 2000 as in 1960. A person in the non-manual group had only around one and three quarters times as much chance of attending HE in 2000 as in 1960. Or looked at in another way, the chances of going to university in 2000 were 2.7 times greater for social group I/II/IIIN than social group IIIM/IV/V, whereas in 1990 the chances had been 3.7, and in 1960 they had been 6.8 (Gorard, 2005a). The situation was better in terms of equity, in this limited respect at least, in 1990 than 1960 and better in 2000 than in 1990.

One of the consequences of this misunderstanding by the DfES is that other evidence relevant to widening participation is then in danger of serious misinterpretation. If a researcher or adviser really believed that the figures in Table 4.2 showed increasing inequality of access by social class then they may conclude,wrongly, that a policy or practice that had actually been helpful was unhelpful or harmful and vice versa. The implications of all this are remarkable. The government, which is the key funder of WP, and many others have little idea about the patterns and trends of under-representation in HE.

Sampling issues

In addition to the absence of comparison groups even in several of the best conducted and best reported studies we reviewed, there are also concerns about the value of some of the samples involved. One example is Francis' (1999) study of the various arguments and discourses that young people draw upon when talking about post-compulsory education. This piece was based upon interview and observation studies of 100 students in three London schools. The sample was drawn from middle and top set Maths and English classes. Not surprisingly, given the nature of the sample, 98 per cent of the pupils wanted to remain in post-16 education. The number wishing to continue was likely to have been lower in the bottom sets who were not included in the research. This is another example of the likely non-participants being left out of research on participation.

Many other studies included similarly large proportions of students who had already made the decision to participate in post-16 (Barrett, 1999) or post-18 education (Brooks, 2003, 2004). Students who chose not to participate were substantially under-researched. There were some studies that specifically set out to examine the decision making process of students who were intending to apply for HE (Mangan *et al*, 2001). Even when all potential students were considered the treatment of the findings tended to follow a pattern where the students are partitioned into those who do or do not intend to participate. Researchers draw the readers' attention to the existence of the non-participants, describe some of the reasons for their choice and then switch the focus to the students who are going to participate.

This degree of attention may be due to the difficulty of locating and including students who choose not to participate in post-compulsory education. Connor (2001) used the Youth Cohort Study to identify a sample of students who had achieved the required grades but did not continue to HE. In total 600 such potential participants were identified but the achieved sample size for the study was only 176 (29%). The problems in identifying those who opt out completely from post-compulsory education was further highlighted in this study when it emerged that 36 per cent of the students previously thought to be non-participants had actually returned to education, possibly after taking a year out. This meant that this study was able to identify only 63 out of a possible 600 students who did not participate in HE even though they had achieved the required grades.

Achieving robust response rates were problematic for several of the larger scale questionnaire surveys. For example, Connor's (2001) postal questionnaire survey of 4,000 undergraduate students had a response rate of 41 per cent. The Sutton Trust's (2002) survey also achieved a response rate of only around 40 per cent. Biggart *et al* (2004) report a 42 per cent response rate in their survey of the educational participation of 17 year-olds in Scotland. In some studies the reporting of response rates and sample sizes was unclear (Croll and Moses, 2003; Mangan *et al*, 2001; Knowles, 1997). All such non-response tends to bias survey results. It is not random and usually tilts the focus of research towards the more academically able and motivated (Payne, 2001). Many surveys are still published without a primary response rate, making any use of their findings ill-advised. In the absence of such information we have to assume the worst and that the response rate is not given because it is low.

For smaller studies there were further problems with the generalisability of some of the findings. This was particularly apparent when results were reported as percentages, masking the small numbers of respondents. For example in Moogan *et al*'s (1999) study 23 per cent of the main sample wanted to attend university to help secure a well paid job. In a sample of just 19 students this represents as few as four students.

Practitioner research

All of the examples so far have come from the academic literature. 'Reflexive' work by practitioners has sometimes been held out as a way of improving the relevance to education research. However it does nothing for the issue of quality being discussed here (Gorard, 2002c). Such work is now common in widening participation research. Our experience is that it is usually conducted without appropriate comparator groups or with no comparator groups at all and with small opportunity samples from the same institutions as the researcher. It typically does not involve interventions, controls or any explicit analysis of patterns or trends. It is not longitudinal in any meaningful sense. There is therefore no way of assessing its propositions or generalising from its results.

Beck *et al* (2004) summarise six such projects, of which three focus on access to education and the barriers to learning that affect recruitment and admissions. Yet all three of these pieces of research involve only accounts of existing students so are unable to address barriers to, or problems of, recruitment because those most affected by the problems have been excluded from the study. The account of the first of these three WP studies contains no description of methods and so gives the reader no idea of sample size nor method of analysis. The report consists of isolated quotations from unknown sources, presenting ideas of unknown prevalence and then a series of implications for policy and practice. The second WP study lists five very broad research questions, including how women see themselves as wives, mothers, learners, workers, and individuals. However, there is no way of assessing how these questions were addressed since no formal methods are presented. The introduction talks about interviews with an undisclosed number of women and the report would have been no longer if the author had simply stated how many women were involved. It presents a list of findings whose quality in relation to the methods we cannot assess. The third WP study lists several ambitious aims including an evaluation of the work of referral agencies. Again, no sample and no methods of data collection or analysis are given. However, it is clear that this study like the others involves talking to the researcher's own students. This gives such a partial view of the role of referral agencies as to be nearly useless or even dangerously misleading.

Conclusion

Many of the research conclusions in the field of widening participation are flawed in two respects. Comparative claims are made without an appropriate comparator. The figures used are not made suitably proportionate. These are general failings of UK educational research which have led to serious misunderstandings in other areas (see Gorard, 2000). For obvious reasons UK educational researchers tend to research learners, who are easy to track, rather than non-learners who are much more expensive to track. This means that adult non-participants are not only routinely excluded from learning but also from the research that is intended to find out why they are excluded.

5

Barriers to participation
in education

Introducing barriers

How do we explain the apparent stratification of access to HE which is described in the first few chapters? To the extent that participation in learning opportunities depends upon the actions of individuals, the official model of how and why people continue in education is based upon a simple application of human capital theory (Coffield, 1999). Individuals are deemed to participate in life-long learning according to their calculation of the net economic benefits to be derived from education and training (Becker, 1975). This leaves two principal issues which government policy must address. First, because an individual's participation in education brings about benefits to society as a whole, it must be ensured that these benefits are internalised into each individual's decision-making. Secondly, the impediments or barriers which prevent people from participating in education who would benefit from doing so must be removed. Points such as these have been made repeatedly in a succession of official and semi-official reports (Dearing, 1997; Fryer, 1997; Department for Trade and Industry, 1998; Kennedy, 1997; National Audit Office, 2002).

The metaphor of barriers to participation is an attractive one that apparently explains differences in patterns of participation between socio-economic groups and also contains its own solution which is removal of the barriers. If it is observed that participation in HE is costly and that potential students from lower income families have lower rates of participation, then it can be hypothesised that cost is a barrier and removal of cost a solution to widening participation. In this chapter we describe some potential barriers that could be producing the existing patterns in participation. The focus is on HE but much of the prior research is based on the same metaphor of barriers applied to all post-compulsory education and training, and this more general area often comes up when searches are conducted involving the term 'barriers'.

Research has suggested several barriers that face potential learners, and that widening post-compulsory participation means recognising and addressing these barriers (Calder, 1993; Burchardt *et al*, 1999). To a large extent the barriers are presaged by the state of adult learning: buildings are not adapted for disability, and there is a shortage of transport for students in rural areas (Hudson, 2005b). There are institutional barriers created by the structure of available opportunities and dispositional barriers in the form of individuals' motivation and attitudes to learning. The most obvious barriers are situational, stemming from the life and lifestyle of the prospective learner (Harrison, 1993). Perhaps the most important of these is the cost of education (McGivney, 1992).

Cost as a barrier

The cost of continuing in education can be direct such as fees, or indirect such as the costs of transport, child care and foregone income (Hand *et al*, 1994). Payment of fees to institutions by instalments is not generally allowed, and many new learners are surprised by the level of other expenses such as examination fees and stationery costs. Benefit entitlement has traditionally been incompatible with formal learning episodes, even when all training costs are met by the individual (Maguire *et al*, 1993). The Employment Service (1991 amended) made clear that

> one of the conditions... to be entitled to unemployment benefit is that you must be . able and willing to take up any job which you are offered immediately. You might not satisfy this rule while you are on a training or education course or programme.

Many people leave learning episodes before completion because of uneven interpretation of the rules by benefits offices.

During the last two decades the costs of higher education in England have gradually been shifting from taxpayers to students and their families. Restrictions on access to unemployment and housing benefits were later accompanied by reduction and then abolition of grants and in 1998 the introduction of means tested contributions towards fees. These rose substantially in September 2006 when HEIs started charging fees of up to £3,000 per year for full-time undergraduates. The movement in England towards a system of income contingent student loans to ensure that HE remains free at the point of consumption followed reforms in Australia, New Zealand and South Africa (Greenaway and Haynes, 2004). Our analysis of the labour market rewards for graduation suggests that participation in HE remains a good investment for the average student (see Chapter Nine). But there have been concerns that this redistribution of the costs of HE will affect marginal entrants with a high aversion to debt and risk and with relatively low expected post-graduation earnings. It has been conjectured that these changes will disproportionately affect potential students from low income families and non-traditional students in general (Education and Employment Committee, 2001; Metcalf, 2005).

Insight into the decision-making process of potential entrants is provided by a survey commissioned by Universities UK (Callender, 2003) of nearly 2,000 UK school and FE college leavers working for HE entry qualifications. The researchers concluded that debt tolerant prospective students were one and a quarter times more likely to enter HE than debt averse students. Those who were most debt averse were from the low income social classes, lone parents and Muslims especially those of Pakistani origin and black and ethnic minority groups. Amongst those still undecided about HE entry the perceived financial barriers were a major cause of their indecision and those from lower income social classes were more likely to mention financial concerns. However, the analysis does not take prior or expected qualification into account.

Metcalf's (2005) study of the initial impact of the introduction of fees concluded that the composition of students had not generally changed in favour of those who can and do absorb the higher debt. Metcalf found that the introduction of fees impacted most on disabled students and students whose families did not provide financial support. These findings suggest that top-up fees are likely to have the greatest effect on participation amongst these groups, especially since disabled students have relatively low expected post-graduation earnings. Whilst the Office for Fair Access requires that HEIs safeguard and promote fair access in the post top-up fees environment, students unsupported by their families are not targeted in OFFA's advice on access agreements.

The literature provides some evidence that there are financial motivations behind some young people's choice not to participate in HE, in particular not wanting to end up in debt. The increase in students continuing to HE has been accompanied by an increase in the number reported to be in debt. The situation is often worse for mature students (Gorard and Taylor, 2001). In

1995, many HE students aged over 26 were over £7,000 in debt (Garner and Imeson, 1996) and the situation worsened with the ending of the older students' allowance so that by 2004 the average debt on graduation was £12,000 (NatWest Money Matters Survey and Barclay's Annual Graduate Survey).

The 2005 Student Experience Report found that the amount of debt that students anticipate on graduation is significantly below the actual debt of current graduates. However, the expected levels of debt of disabled students and those from working-class backgrounds were 37 per cent and 46 per cent respectively higher than the average £10,000 debt. The same survey found that about 30 per cent of current students were seriously worried about the debts incurred in university study. Metcalf (2005) notes the increase from 29 per cent to 34 per cent in the number of students expressing regrets about going to university since the introduction of tuition fees. She concludes that the effects of fee introduction were both to increase expected student debt and the degree of inequality of debt of those leaving higher education. A common factor amongst studies categorising students' motivation to enter higher education is finance – which is particularly pertinent given the current climate of mounting higher education costs (Gerrard and Roberts, 2006).

McGrath and Millen (2004) reported six out of 21 respondents citing financial reasons for withdrawing once they had received an offer of a place, mostly before receiving their A-level results. Financial concerns are mediated by personal and private reasons, such as having family responsibilities (Connor, 2001). Many students seemed resigned to ending up in debt; it was a consequence of being a student. There was some unconvincing evidence that financial concerns were more of an issue for students from poorer homes. Several studies queried the levels of financial literacy among prospective students (Helmsley-Brown, 1999) but it was not clear whether this was actually a barrier for the respondents. Competing responsibilities and preference for earning money were key self-reported reasons for non-participation among potential applicants (Collier *et al*, 2003) and potential entrants to HE perceived time or financial commitment to be the main barriers to their participation (Ulrich, 2004). Additional factors were identified by Schuller *et al* (1997) in the form of employer support for those undertaking study whilst in employment, which could be financial or time off. The importance of future employment was raised by Kay and Sundaraj (2004), who found that a desire to change career paths or to improve their career prospects was the predominant motivation amongst mature students. They also noted that these motivations were reflected in the students' choice of course.

Glover *et al* (2002) conducted a survey with 400 students on commencement and on completion of their university course and found that economic motivation was more important to students than the pursuit of knowledge. The authors argue that simply graduating from University is not a sufficient basis for continued personal and institutional investment in HE and that as a result HE courses will be expected to be increasingly directed towards future employment. Winn (2002) argues that efforts to enhance student motivation through the use of teaching, learning and assessment strategies will have limited effect unless the Government targets effective financial support to students with child care responsibilities and provides greater incentives for part-time study.

In all studies that examined this aspect of student life, working part-time to reduce the overall cost of study was found to be difficult. For example, participants in Bamber and Tett's (2000) investigation stated that part-time employment could act as a barrier to full engagement with their degree, although the organisers of their course had structured timetabling to account for part-time work commitments. Participants who had worked part-time as students, referred to in Noble (2004), generally worked more than the maximum twelve hours recommended by the Select Committee on Education and Employment, which led to difficulties in their keeping on track with university demands. Likewise, by the end of Walker's (1999) longitudinal project, two-thirds of participants were in part-time employment, many working for more than 20 hours a week. Only one individual was in a job that related to his/her course. Unfortunately, the majority of students who worked part-time still experienced financial struggles.

Case study material presented in Thomas *et al* (2001) suggested that for some individuals part-time work was essential to enable them to complete their course, whilst for others it was undertaken to fund their attempts to fit in with a middle-class lifestyle. Having little money compared with friends who worked full time was depicted as a difficulty, as was returning to a student income for older learners who had been used to earning a wage (Thomas, 2002). Research also reports that the pressure of having to work could lead to missing lectures which then played a role in some people's decision to leave university.

The impact of bursaries
The UK Universities study (Callender, 2003) concluded that the level of funds available to HE students through the student support system was a barrier to widening participation. Uncertainty about access to discretionary funding

was a deterrent to participation. The complexity of student funding was found to impede entry and made the interpretation of information difficult, especially for older, low income students with dependents. Forthcoming changes to fees and student funding are likely to further increase the overall complexity of the financial decisions facing HE entrants in England. Metcalf (2005) reported that the system of hardship grants had not equalised finances across the student body. Students in receipt of hardship grants were expecting to incur a one sixth higher debt than the average on completion of their studies. However, West *et al* (2003) found that the award of a bursary had a positive psychological impact by reducing students' fear of debt.

Manski (1989) has pointed out that the theoretical effect of financial aid on educational outcomes in general and retention in particular is ambiguous. By lowering the cost of education retention is likely to be enhanced but by encouraging participation amongst less academically prepared students financial aid may also lower retention. Previous research in the US has failed to reach a consensus on this issue (Kerkvliet and Nowell, 2005) and little research has so far been undertaken in the UK. In a pioneering small scale study Hatt *et al* (2005a, 2005b) found that students at two English HEIs who received bursaries were more likely to complete their first year successfully than non-bursary students from low income backgrounds; bursaries eased the transition into HE, altered the students' perception of their university favourably and enhanced their commitment to succeed. However, Hatt *et al's* study was of two modern universities and Kerkvliet and Nowell (2005) found that grants had encouraged retention in an undergraduate commuter university but not in a research-intensive residential university in the US. This shows the need to consider the impact of bursary schemes in different types of higher educational institutions and different types of entrants.

A further key issue concerns whether bursaries are more effective if they are allocated on the basis of prior academic performance (merit-aid) or low family income (need-based aid). Since the early 1990s sixteen states in the US have established broad based merit-aid programmes providing scholarships to hundreds of thousands of students. These programmes typically waive tuition and fees at all public HEIs in a student's home state and, unlike the National Merit Scholarship scheme, these state programmes typically require recipients to have only a modest previous academic performance. An analysis of merit-aid programmes in seven states by Dynarski (2003) indicated that they increased the attendance probability of college aged youths by 5-7 percentage points whilst shifting students towards four-year schools and away from two-year schools. These programmes tended to have a stronger impact on the college attendance rates of blacks and Hispanics. In contrast, research suggests that needs-based aid programmes in the US, such as the Pell Grant scheme, have more modest and sometimes insignificant effects on participation and that these have recently been displaced by merit-based programmes (Singell *et al*, 2005).

On the other hand

Despite such indirect evidence of the importance of finance as a barrier, studies in post-compulsory education more generally do not find the same thing. Whatever those participating may say about finance, and it obviously has not totally prevented them from accessing education, non-participants usually cite other non-financial reasons for not continuing with formal education (Selwyn *et al*, 2006). A recent survey by the Adult Learning Inspectorate shows that the widespread provision of free tuition for adults previously without level 2 qualifications did not increase numbers. Rather it changed who did what where (Lee, 2006a). This attraction or re-direction of the usual suspects is common. Is there any similar evidence from HE?

Dearden *et al* (2004a) provide an aggregate analysis of the impact of credit constraints on educational choices in the UK. They attempt to estimate both the share of individuals not staying on at the end of compulsory schooling and those qualified for entry but who are not attaining an HE qualification because of short-term credit constraints. They generate this estimate by comparing participation rates across the parental income distribution and after controlling for a number of observed measures of early family and environmental influences. Given data limitations, they viewed these estimates as an upper bound on the share of individuals genuinely facing short-run credit constraints. Using the NCDS58 and BCS70 cohorts they concluded that at age 16 there was a 7 per cent gap in staying-on rates between individuals coming from families in the top income quartile and those from the bottom income quartile, for the 1970 cohort only. In terms of HE attainment the gap was much lower and may not represent a real difference at all. Therefore finance alone is unlikely to be an important factor in generating stratified access to HE. Dearden *et al* conclude that if these patterns from 1986 still hold, then policy should target student decision-making at age 16. Early indications are that the Education Maintenance Allowance seems to be having a significant impact on increasing participation in post-compulsory education, particularly amongst males and those from the poorest socio-economic backgrounds (Dearden *et al*, 2005).

There is some international evidence on the effects of a deferred fee system on widening participation. In Australia, where the income contingent charging system dates back to 1989, the proportion of young people from the lowest socio-economic backgrounds attending HE has remained largely unchanged, whilst the overall participation rate has increased (Chapman and Ryan, 2002). This suggests that an income contingent loan system may be fairly neutral in its impact upon widening participation. Findings from surveys of prospective Australian students (James, 2002) and of existing students (Long and Hayden, 2001) were generally similar to those reported for the UK. Similarly, in Wales, HESA statistics show a steady long-term rise in the number of first degree undergraduates from 1995 to 2003 despite the introduction of up-front tuition fees in 1999. The same is true of the increase in student numbers in Wales both before and after the re-introduction of grants in 2001 (Taylor and Gorard, 2005).

Table 5.1 opposite shows a gradual year on year increase in the number of Welsh-domiciled students participating in HE. This represents a 19 per cent increase between 1995/96 and 2002/03. The data include the year that up-front first degree and undergraduate tuition fees were introduced in Wales (1998/99) and the year that the Assembly Learning Grants (ALG) and the Financial Contingency Fund (FCF) were established by the Welsh Assembly Government (2002/03). The only year that saw a fall in the number of Welsh-domiciled students was 1999/00, the year following the introduction of up-front tuition fees. However, we should not attribute this difference directly to fees because the previous year had shown the greatest single increase in participation on record, such that if the years 1998/99 and 1999/00 are averaged then the graph becomes a continuous straight rise since 1997/98 and continuing for as many years as data are available. What may have happened is that uncertainty over fees encouraged some people to enter HE immediately who in other years may have waited. This caused a one-year jump in growth. Once the uncertainty was clarified the trend in rising participation reverted to normal but took one year to recover because of the absence of those new students who had actually started the year before.

There is no way of telling from such HESA statistics how many potential students are deterred from studying by the costs involved (Gorard and Taylor, 2001). The proportion of students leaving or completing their course who report finance as the problem is low: around 0.6 per cent or 148 students per year in Wales. This is in relation to what is reputedly one of the lowest dropout rates in the world, second only to HE in Japan. Once again this data refers only to those who have entered HEIs and therefore provides no direct evi-

Table 5.1: Growth in Welsh-domiciled students 1995/96 to 2002/03

Year	Number of students
1995/96	25,511
1996/97	n/a
1997/98	25,143
1998/99	28,051
1999/00	26,853
2000/01	29,739
2001/02	30,060
2002/03	30,574

Source: HESA

Note: First year undergraduates

dence on the importance of financial constraints in deterring HE participation. However, a study of participation rates between 1994 and 2000 (HEFCE, 2005) also found no evidence that the introduction of tuition fees and the replacement of grants with loans had significantly affected entrant behaviour or patterns.

As with Gorard and Taylor (2001) Table 5.2 on page 60 shows that finance is not a key factor in non-completion of HE courses, accounting for less than 3 per cent of all early leavers. The most likely explanation for this is that because of the link between high level qualifications and socio-economic advantage, many of the potential students eligible and qualified for entry to HE are relatively advantaged (Forsyth and Furlong, 2003). There is not a large body of socio-economically disadvantaged people who are currently eligible for entry to HE but do not participate, although financial considerations might influence their choice of subject, length of course, and institution. It is becoming clear that HEIs in England which offer the largest bursaries to new students are falling behind in terms of applications. Finance is neither a complete barrier nor a complete solution to participation.

Time and travel as barriers

Loss of time to have a social life can be another cost of learning (McGivney, 1990; FEU, 1993). Adult education may have begun to suffer not so much from lack of leisure time but from the multiplicity of opportunities available for that time (Kelly, 1992). Taking a course often involves an adjustment in lifestyle which may be possible for some individuals but is more of a problem for those with dependants or who are in long-term relationships. Partners as

Table 5.2: Percentage of reasons for non-completing Welsh-domiciled students 1995/96 to 2002/03

Year	1995/96	1997/98	1998/99	1999/00	2000/01	2001/02	2002/03
Other personal reasons	32	30	30	29	29	27	35
Other	22	14	14	16	13	14	24
Unknown	18	21	28	27	27	19	15
Academic failure	12	16	14	13	17	27	12
Health reasons	4	4	3	3	3	3	2
Written off after lapse in time	4	7	3	3	3	3	4
Financial reasons	3	3	3	3	3	2	2
Gone into employment	3	4	4	4	3	3	4
Death	0	0	0	0	1	0	0
Exclusion	0	0	3	2	2	1	2

Source: HESA

well as children tend to reduce the time available for learning in womens' lives more than in men's (Abroms and Goldscheider, 2002). For some women, even those who had been successful at school and who had clear plans about how their career and life would unfold, further opportunities were often put on hold because of children so that they 'essentially replicated the employment patterns of women of an earlier generation' (p265). The most vulnerable women from the most disadvantaged backgrounds face the greatest barrier in terms of time. All such costs are clearly more restrictive for the poor and for those with other commitments such as a young family.

Barriers such as transport also apply to all forms of participation. In one small study of one area and one FE college a major reason for not continuing with study was given as distance to the nearest FE college (Hramiak, 2001). For the ethnic minority women involved it was more about psychological distance from family responsibilities than the actual travel involved. Dhillon's (2004) focus groups with adults learning at learndirect centres found that learning on the doorstep, meaning proximity to home and convenience for travel, were strong factors influencing their participation in this type of learning, coupled with the flexibility that this learning environment offered. The learners valued the opening hours, the lack of a specific requirement to attend at pre-specified times and the ability to arrange to drop in for learning at times to fit in with their other commitments. Dodgson and Bolam (2002) found that ICT was widely used in the six universities in the north east of England to improve the flexibility of learning opportunities. Studies such as these are only based on self-reports and do not provide evidence that ICT attracts new students into HE in the UK who would not otherwise have enrolled or that it makes their retention and success more likely.

Osborne (2003), drawing on the work in Australia by Postle et al (2002) recognises the potential limitations for access to ICT-based distance learning by students from lower socio-economic groups. The cost of an internet service provider and the time it takes to download material could be prohibitive. This barrier is reportedly reduced by learndirect centres. However, a major study by Selwyn et al (2006) showed that even studies such as these are biased in their use only of participants in education. From the point of view of non-participants, virtual learning and distance provision relying on ICT reinforces the barriers to participation that it is meant to overcome.

Motivation
Even where provision is available, awareness of opportunities may be patchy for some parts of the population (Taylor and Spencer, 1994), giving many a

feeling that 'you are on your own'. Barriers of any kind are harder for the less motivated prospective student. Lack of provision of learning for leisure and at home, with the focus on formal public arenas such as work mean that learners may be perceived as younger, better educated, and from higher in-come groups than they really are (Edwards *et al*, 1993). To some extent this image becomes self-realising. People with these characteristics tend to be selected for learning so that social practice becomes reproductive and educa-tion is seen as middle class and 'not for the likes of us'. A poor experience of previous educational episodes may create an obstacle to continuing educa-tion (Taylor and Spencer, 1994). If initial education has not provided basic study skills such as numeracy, this is a further barrier. An estimated six million adults in Britain may have difficulty with writing or numeracy and one sixth of adults have problems with basic literacy. These deficiencies pass through generations of the same families (DfEE, 1998), becoming a reproduc-tive determinant of adult non-learning.

The influence of lack of motivation to learn may be underestimated by litera-ture concentrating on the more easily visible barriers such as cost and entry qualifications. (McGivney, 1993). Many people display an incorrigible reluc-tance to learn formally. In fact 21 per cent of adults form a hard core of non-participants who remain outside all attempts to reach them (Titmus, 1994). If all the barriers were removed for them by provision of free tuition and con-venient travel, they would still not want to learn. They have no desire and given greater leisure time would want to 'just waste it'. Self-identity in Britain may be more strongly linked to a job than it is in other countries, where a greater emphasis is placed on learning (Bynner, 1998). Lack of drive thus be-comes the most important barrier of all since it is seen as easy to get a job instead and qualifications are seen as useless anyway. Some young people do not even bother to find out what their public examination results are since they are only concerned with getting a job (Banks *et al*, 1992). Qualifications may even be seen as antagonistic to getting a job, and only concerned with entry to more education. Learning is something which is done early in life as a preparation but with no relevance to the world of adults (Harrison, 1993). Such attitudes may form early in the links between school and family expec-tations (see Chapter Six).

On the other hand several studies have found no difference between learners and non-learners in their attitudes to full-time education (Park, 1994). Dif-ferences in class culture are no longer such a barrier to post-16 or post-18 participation (Furlong, 2005). Perhaps the benefits of participation are more widely acknowledged while the actual culture of HE/FE has converged with mainstream culture. Most people acknowledge the benefit of learning although learners are more likely to report non-material benefits but at least a third, especially volunteer self-funders and the unemployed, do not see learning as having any positive effect on job prospects.

Institutional barriers

The institutional barriers to participation in post-compulsory education often come from the procedures of the providing organisations in terms of advertisement, entry procedures, timing and scale of provision and general lack of flexibility. Colleges of FE have traditionally assumed a 17 year-old norm and are having to adapt to more flexible opportunities for learning. People want to fit learning around other tasks of equal importance in their lives since they cannot always get time off. They often have interrupted patterns of participation and diverse progression routes (Gorard and Rees, 2002). Non-completion of some courses is so high that it must be partly seen as an indictment of the quality of provision at all levels: schools, further education, and youth training. Dropout is commonly caused by people discovering that they are on the wrong course with nearly half of FE students in one survey feeling that they had made a mistake (FEU, 1993). Part of the blame for this lies with the institutions which do not give appropriate initial guidance (Maguire *et al*, 1993). Many learners are disappointed by the lack of help available in choosing a course and in staying on it. Such barriers are considered further in Chapter Eight.

Part of the cause of lack of participation may be lack of appropriate provision (Banks *et al*, 1992). Even those who are studying may not have found what they actually wanted (Park, 1994). This is particularly true of non-work related training and learning for leisure, and is reinforced by the current emphasis on certified courses, heavily backed up by the incentives in the funding arrangements to provide accreditation of all adult education. Not only does this deny some people the opportunity to learn new interests and make new friends, it denies returners an easy and non-threatening entry route back into education.

Conclusion

Overall, the idea of barriers to learning is elegant both as explanation of the differences in participation and as a suggestion for their amelioration. However, there is little clear evidence of their impact in creating stratified access and a consequent danger that they tend towards tautological non-explanations. The relatively low level of participation from lower income groups, for example, gives rise to the explanation that cost is a barrier. If this is so, then removal or reduction of the cost should lead to increased participation from these groups. This is the logic underlying grants, fees remission, and means-tested bursaries but there is little direct evidence that these approaches work differentially well for the groups for whom they are intended. Removing the apparent barriers to participation is not as easy as it sounds (Selwyn *et al*, 2006), and this casts doubt on the value of the concept of barriers as an explanation for non-participation. It leads us instead to a fuller consideration of the personal, social and economic determinants of participation and non-participation in education.

6

A life-course approach:
early life and schooling

The loose pattern of social and economic under-representation of some groups of potential students in HE is already apparent among those with pre-university qualifications equivalent to UK National Qualification Framework (NQF) level 3, such as two or more A-levels. This pattern is based on differential staying-on rates in schools and colleges (NIACE, 2000). Many of those who stay on in education after the age of 16 to take level 3 qualifications do so to try and get into HE. These staying-on rates are heavily based on level 2 qualifications, and so on.

This leads us to two important considerations. First, the solutions to any problems facing WP are not only to be found in HE itself. The solution to educational inequality may not be found in education at all. Second, to understand these patterns we have to take a life course view of participation. Therefore, the rest of this book is presented in life-long order from pre-university life to the transition to HE, through attendance at HE to life after HE. In this chapter we cover issues relevant to the stage of life before attending HE.

The determinants of participation at birth

Individuals with similar social backgrounds from different birth cohorts show differing tendencies to participate in education and training. When they were born determines their relationship to changing opportunities for learning and social expectations (Rees *et al*, 2006). Time may represent a variety of factors such as objective changes in local opportunities, economic development, the increasing formalisation of training, the antagonism between learning and work, the age and maturity of an individual at any period and the changing social expectations of the role of women.

Similarly, where people are born and brought up shapes their social ex-pectations and access to specifically local opportunities. Those who have lived in the most economically disadvantaged areas are least likely to parti-cipate in life-long learning. This may be partly to do with the relative social capital of those in differing areas or differences in local opportunities for learning. However, those who have moved between regions are even more likely to participate than those remaining in the more advantaged localities. Those who are geographically mobile tend to be participants in adult educa-tion or training while those who remain in one area, sometimes over several generations tend to be non-participants (Gorard and Rees, 2002).

The sex of an individual can make a considerable difference. Men consis-tently report more formal post-16 learning than women. Although the situa-tion is changing, these changes are different for each sex. Older women are less likely than men of the same age to have participated in learning life-long but younger women are now more likely to have undertaken extended initial education. Extended initial education is now relatively gender neutral, even over-representing women, while later education or training is increasingly the preserve of males. In one study any choices which were made are per-ceived to have been heavily constrained by external circumstances (Gorard *et al*, 2001b). Many older women describe the ways in which the learning opportunities available to them were limited by local employment, social ex-pectations or by a 'forced altruism' with respect to family commitments. Even younger women respondents provide similar accounts (Beck *et al*, 2006).

Even at birth, an individual's characteristics and circumstances predispose them to future participation or non-participation in formal episodes of edu-cation.

Early-life determinants of participation

In a review of evidence on the impact of parental education on early life, Fein-stein *et al* (2004) showed that key influences on a child's educational attain-ment in the early years include parental education and income. Occupational status and family size are also relevant but the causal pathway is less clear here. Once parental income and education are accounted for, measures such as family structure, maternal employment or teenage motherhood are not important as determinants of child attainment. One explanation for this pattern relies on an assumption of the inheritability of talent. If parents are talented then they may be more likely to have higher levels of attainment and income and to pass this talent on to their children. Another explanation would be that the income and education of parents affects their beliefs, values, aspirations and attitudes, which are transmitted to their children via proximal interaction. Whatever the cause, the solution would, according to Rawls (1971), be the same and consists of diverting extra help and resources to the most disadvantaged in society.

Family background is most obviously influential in material terms but also in terms of what is understood to be the natural form of participation. In one large study, a number of those who had participated actively in post-school learning said that this was what was normatively prescribed within the family or the wider community, rather than their own active choice (Gorard *et al*, 1999b). Families are universally acknowledged to be a key determinant of educational performance in primary and secondary schooling and, by extension, in higher education too. In compulsory education similar educational routes within families are widely recognised. For example, the occupational or class background of parents is routinely used as an explanatory factor in analyses of educational attainment or progress through the compulsory educational system (Halsey *et al*, 1980). Similarly, the influences of ethnic background are recognised as being mediated through families (Wilson, 1987).

It is striking that this framework of family influences on educational performance is rarely extended to the analysis of participation in life-long learning. The few studies which have been conducted have found weaker links between the involvement of parents and children in education and training through the life course than between their early qualifications (Cervero and Kirkpatrick, 1990). Indeed, the correlations between parental education and the child's later participation in education in the longitudinal model created by Yang (1998) are so low that, even when combined with many other predictor variables, such as school attainment and attitudinal variables, only 23 per cent to 30 per cent of the variance in participation is explained although this model only caters for adults aged from 16 to 32. Gorard *et al* (1999b), on the other hand, find that almost half of the children who are lifelong learners have parents who are life-long learners themselves (46%). Similarly, more than half of the children who are non-participants have parents who are non-participants (61%). It is clear that, for whatever reason, patterns of participation to some extent run in families.

Merrell and Tymms (2005) considered data from a variety of pre-school schemes which were intended to overcome the negative relationship between the economic deprivation of children and their early skills such as language learning. These interventions are generally beneficial in the sense that there is a slight advantage in attending such a scheme rather than not, although in the absence of random allocation we cannot tell whether this is a volunteer or motivational effect. However, such schemes do not ameliorate the weak relationship between deprivation and language skill.

Overall, the experience of early family life does nothing to equalise an individual's chances of continuing with formal education when given the choice. And there is no clear evidence of the success of pre-school interventions.

Initial schooling as a determinant of participation

The experiences gained during initial schooling are another important factor in shaping long-term orientations towards learning and in providing the qualifications necessary to access many forms of further and higher education. State funded compulsory education for all children is an intervention intended to equalise life opportunities and remedy inequalities such as the number of books at home or the reading ability of parents. However, because this intervention is universal in the UK and is now so mature, it is very hard to decide what effect it has had on educational mobility. Official school improvement policy is now based on contextualised value-added analyses which, in addition to facing scientific challenges, make it impossible to decide whether schools are successfully compensating for early disadvantage or not (Gorard, 2006b). On an appropriately sceptical reading, it is difficult to find any evidence that less bold initial education interventions since the 1944 Education Act have had much impact on patterns of inequality. In general, taken over historical time periods, both the quality and equality of education in England have improved (e.g. Gorard, 2000). However, what is largely absent from these trends are abrupt or localised changes attributable to specific changes in educational practice (Gorard, 2006b).

This is a common theme across sectors and ages of education. Many initiatives are ineffective, either by not being associated with any improvement (Gorard et al, 2002a; Gorard and Smith, 2004) or by being associated with an improvement that was happening anyway (Tymms et al, 2005). Area-based initiatives, such as Academies (Gorard, 2005b) or Action Zones (Power et al, 2005), have no clearly desirable effect in terms of targeting those most in need (Parkinson, 1998). Even where initiatives are beneficial in absolute terms they are not especially effective in reducing inequality. In some cases the more advantaged students gain more from such interventions, leading to a temporary increase in inequality.

Success or failure at school affects the choice of what to do post-16 and there is even a school effect on that choice (Pustjens et al, 2004). Experience of school lays the foundation for what could be an enduring learner identity. It is interesting how those who took the 11-plus examination testified to its major and often traumatic effects (Gorard and Rees, 2002). For respondents too young to have gone through the tripartite system, although success and failure are less starkly defined, they still identify positive experiences of schooling as crucial determinants of enduring attitudes towards subsequent learning. Those who failed at school often view post-school learning of all kinds as irrelevant to their needs and capacities. Participation in further, higher and continuing education is not seen as a realistic possibility and even work-based learning is viewed as unnecessary. Whilst this attitude is not confined to those whose school careers were less successful in conventional terms, it is almost universally held amongst this group (Selwyn *et al*, 2006).

Learning trajectories

It is important to be clear about the strength of the life-long pattern of inequality in education and its transmission across generations of the same family (Gorard *et al*, 1999b; San-Segundo and Valiente, 2003). Early context factors are closely related to early educational attainment, which is related to staying-on rates at age 16, and to patterns of traditional-age participation in HE. There is a pattern of typical learning trajectories which can effectively encapsulate the complexity of individual education and training biographies. Some people leave formal education at the earliest opportunity. Some of these leavers return to formal learning as adults but a high proportion do not. Other people continue into extended initial education but never return to formal learning later. Others remain in contact with formal learning for a large proportion of their lives. Which of these trajectories, from life-long non-participation to life-long learning, an individual takes can be accurately predicted on the basis of characteristics which are known by the time they reach school-leaving age.

This does not imply that people do not have choices or that life crises have little impact but rather that these choices and crises occur within a framework of opportunities, influences and social expectations that are determined by the resources which they derive from their background and upbringing (Gorard and Rees, 2002). More importantly, an individual's capacity to take up whatever learning opportunities are available can be constrained by their previous history so that trajectories do not simply reflect the objective structure of access to learning opportunities. The selection of individual educational experiences reflects learner identities which are built up over the life of the individual.

All the factors dealt with so far reflect characteristics of respondents which are determined relatively early in the life course. Gorard and Rees (2002) entered variables measuring five determinants, time, place, sex, family and initial schooling, into a logistic regression function in the order in which they occur in real life. Those characteristics which are set very early in life, such as age, sex and family background, predict later learning trajectories with 75 per cent accuracy. Adding the variables representing initial schooling increases the accuracy of prediction to 90 per cent. One possible explanation for this re-markable finding is that family poverty, lack of role models and a sense of 'not for us', coupled with poor experiences of initial schooling can create a life-long attitude to learning or a negative learner identity. In this case the obvious barriers such as cost, time and travel are largely irrelevant. In the same way that most of the population is not deterred from higher education by lack of finance, so most non-participants in basic skills training are not put off by barriers but by their lack of interest in something that seems alien and im-posed. To deal with this we must first understand it. In the relative social and economic situation for any individual the choice not to participate could be completely rational. We need to revise any complacency that the existing set-up for learning is appropriate for all and that the reluctant learner need only be lured back on track.

Replicated analyses, conducted with several different datasets totalling 10,000 adults across the entire UK, have shown that the same determinants of post-compulsory participation appear each time (Gorard *et al,* 2003). These findings are robust. The key social determinants which predict life-long parti-cipation in formal learning involve time, place, sex, family and initial school-ing. Such results offer important correctives to the conventional view of parti-cipation in life-long learning. This conventional view is the accumulation thesis which prioritises the determining influence of earlier adult behaviour on what education and training individuals undertake later in their lives. As Tuijnman (1991) puts it, the best single predictor of later participation in edu-cation and training is earlier participation. Nevertheless, it is important to note that the correlations are low. Therefore 'the life-long education cycle cannot be comprehended without the inclusion and analysis of other factors influencing the accumulation of educational experiences' (p283). These other factors include area of residence, sex, and parental occupation, as well as parental education (Gerber and Hout, 1995; Zhou *et al,* 1998). The accumu-lation thesis is much weaker and the role of an individual's background is much stronger than has been argued conventionally. The reasons why early learners are more often life-long learners could be the same as the reason for their early participation and based on family background, sex, and regional conditions. This would be as convincing an explanation as the accumulation model. For example, while initial educational success may be a good indicator of later participation the success itself can be partly predicted by social and family background in the model of trajectories proposed here.

Inequalities in HE participation appear in terms of age, place, sex, ethnicity, first language, parental and sibling social class, parental education, type of school attended, housing tenure, health, disability, criminal activity, learning difficulties, family structure and religious background. However, precisely the same inequalities are apparent in patterns of initial education and in patterns of other forms of adult education which recur in succeeding generations of the same family. These inequalities are so pervasive that it might be misleading to think of them as educational problems at all. At an aggregated level, Gorard *et al* (2004b) conducted an exploratory factor analysis for the Basic Skills Agency with a basket of indicators of relative disadvantage and found that nearly all of them were expressing the same underlying factor. These indicators included:

- attainment in Maths, Science and English at Key Stages 1, 2 and 3
- GCSE benchmark of five or more grades A*-C
- the number of school leavers with no qualifications
- the number of adults of working-age and of all ages with no recognised qualification
- indicators of childhood disadvantage
- eligibility for Free School Meals at primary and secondary school
- child poverty
- children living in households on benefit
- protected and registered children
- where people were born
- local economic activity rates
- the proportion of those on benefit
- unemployment rates at age 16
- long-term and overall unemployment
- social housing

- household income

- health scores

- poor health

- life expectancy

- child mortality

- total absences from school

- all indicators of teenage pregnancy

- the proportion of abortions.

Put more simply inequalities in initial education could be viewed as simply a manifestation of profound multiple social disadvantage.

Transitions at 16+

What happens at age 16 could be crucial to our understanding of inequalities in HE because 'many 16 year-olds who stay on do so to gain qualifications for higher education' (Raffe *et al*, 2001, p46). The students themselves focus more on choice at 16 than at 18 (McLinden, 2003). If true this has two important implications for WP. For many the decision to enter HE is therefore effectively taken several years beforehand. The local provision, its visibility and the take-up of HE could be an important influence on staying-on rates at 16.

In the UK the school-leaving age was raised in 1972 from age 15 to 16, producing an inevitable but not total increase in staying on in education past 15. A very similar growth in post-16 participation took place in the 1990s despite their being no legal compulsion. The Youth Cohort Study shows a steep growth in full-time education post-16 after 1989 (Payne, 1998). However, this is largely a question of robbing Peter to pay Paul because government funded training showed an almost equivalent drop over the same period from 24 per cent of 16 year-olds in 1989 to 12 per cent in 1994. Even today increases in staying-on rates in FE often replace work-based training, and growth in full-time leads to a decline in part-time participation (Denholm and Macleod, 2003). The total proportion of the 16-year-old cohort remaining in education, government schemes and employment-based training combined has remained almost constant for decades, even though the balance between the three routes varies according to the local history of funding and availability. And the proportion remaining in education and training continues to be stratified in terms of social class, ethnicity and region.

The majority of students in studies of post-16 choice want to remain in education to the next level, either post-16 or post-18, partly because of the inherent bias in UK education research towards researching the best educated. For example, a study of the post-16 destinations of 3,000 participants in the Northern Ireland Curriculum Cohort study found that 70 per cent of students remained in education post-16 while around 13 per cent entered work-related training, 8 per cent found employment, with around 2 per cent unemployed and 4 per cent whose destinations were unknown (Moor *et al*, 2004). The likelihood of remaining in education post-16 depended to a large extent on prior GCSE/GNVQ performance. Even in Archer and Yamashita's (2003) study of twenty lower ability year 11 students from an inner London school, eleven students stated their desire to remain in education post-16 despite being identified by their teachers as 'unlikely to continue'. Of those who do not stay in education immediately, few (around 4% in Raffe *et al*, 2001) returned in the second or subsequent years. Those returning are generally the best qualified, with the highest level of parental education and support (Hammer, 2003). And those who are least likely to participate in any phase also appear to become the most likely to drop out (Walker *et al*, 2004).

This means that post-16 participation is stratified both in relation to non-participation and in relation to the routes followed by different socio-economic groups. Young people who do not like school often prefer the culture of FE which allows them to dress how they want, treats them like adults, involves activities other than reading and writing, and has an element of real adult life. An increase in flexible options which encourage out of school teaching for those who do not like school may therefore reinforce class, race and gender segregation in terms of different tracks (Ecclestone, 2006). Currently, vocational education can become almost anything that engages low-achieving students and so its provision could increase their segregation from high achievers on different courses.

A key indicator of whether or not individuals chose to stay on is success in school examinations (Thomas *et al*, 2001; Croll and Moses, 2003; Howieson and Ianelli, 2003). Watson and Church (2003) found that potential WP students in year 10 were not likely to reach even the GCSE benchmark necessary for sixth-form study but were still positive about participating in HE. They had the usual concerns about barriers such as finance and dropout from HE but since they were unlikely to gain suitable qualifications they might not be allowed to continue post-16. The level of qualification at 16+ clearly predicts a student's educational pathway and later employment status (McIntosh, 2004). In this case the role of purported barriers to participation, such as cost, can only be minimal. There is some consensus about the reasons students give for wanting to participate, with access to a better job being a key reason at all stages (Francis, 1999; Barrett, 1999; Moogan *et al*, 1999; Sutton Trust, 2002; Connor, 2001; Moor *et al*, 2004). Other reasons include achieving certain qualifications, the perceived usefulness of education, the importance of being educated and the possibility of higher earnings.

Peers may exert a certain amount of influence over the decision to remain in education, particularly post-16 and over the choice of subject (Mangan *et al*, 2001; Thomas *et al*, 2001; Thomas and Webber, 2001; Lumby *et al*, 2003). There was a limited role for schools and teaching staff in influencing students' decisions about whether to participate (Thomas *et al*, 2003), and this mainly involved alerting students to the possibility of continuing to higher education (Moogan *et al*, 1999). Parents were frequently seen as the major influence and encouragement in shaping students' decisions to participate in post-compulsory education (Sutton Trust, 2002; McGrath and Millen, 2004; Helmsley-Brown, 1999; Archer and Yamashita, 2003), and also in in choosing where to study and what courses to follow (Brooks, 2003, 2004). Often the parents had little experience of HE but were still key participants in the decision making process (Moogan *et al*, 1999). Biggart *et al* (2004) reported that parents were the single biggest source of advice on continuation (48%) and that the reasons given for prospective choices were strongly linked to parents' occupational class. Students from manual and unskilled backgrounds were more likely to want to leave school, having 'had enough' and perhaps having been offered a job. It is possible that the promotional material produced by post-16 providers, intended to encourage participation, actually works as a form of occupational class marker (Maguire *et al*, 1999).

Pre-entry interventions for school pupils
What can educators do to change things at this stage and to reduce subsequent stratification in HE? Most HEIs in England make presentations in schools, undertake visits to reinforce school links and even arrange parent-focused activities with the aim of widening participation (Pennell *et al*, 2005). However, there is almost no evaluation of these activities. Most evaluation takes the form of self-reported aspirations of those who are involved in the interventions, without a comparator group. For example, Thomas and Slack (1999, 2000) found that interventions in Year 9 had only a limited impact in influencing future decisions about education and training but had a greater impact in relation to career aspirations. Unfortunately, like much of the research on school interventions to widen participation, this study explored

staff and pupils' perceptions of interventions, as opposed to their actual effectiveness. None of the research addresses the efficiency or cost-effectiveness of the interventions which is a major blind spot for the whole field.

This limited research on school-based interventions suggests that to have the greatest positive effect on young people:

- Targeting has to be explicit and overseen by the intervention rather than the school, otherwise the intended beneficiaries may be excluded and the more likely beneficiaries included (Woodrow *et al*, 1998). Some evidence suggests that some pupils are better able to take advantage of activities and that without careful targeting the gap between groups of pupils may actually increase as a result.

- Activities have to be of interest and relevance to the young people (Thomas and Slack, 1999)

- Activities need to be interactive and engaging. Greater Merseyside Aimhigher (2003) found that practical, hands on activities, project/ problem based activities, team work in small groups with an undergraduate facilitator were more engaging, in the view of staff and pupils.

- School cultures and activities have to reinforce widening participation interventions (Morris *et al*, 2005a, 2005b)

- Activities need to involve parents: in Year 9, parents (Thomas and Slack, 2000) and particularly mothers (McLinden, 2003) were considered the main influence on young people's decision making.

Most HEIs hold summer schools as a WP activity (Pennell *et al*, 2005). As with school-based interventions, much of the research about summer schools and residential experiences has focused on students' perceptions of their experiences and their intended actions rather than on outcomes in terms of participation, retention or qualification. No data is presented about how many pupils subsequently enter HE or how this differs from the progression rates of non-participating students. According to Pennell *et al* (2005) most HEIs have a student ambassador scheme, run student mentoring programmes and organise school pupil tutoring by undergraduates. Given this volume of activity, and the strong claims made for it (Knox and McGillvray, 2005; McLinden, 2003), relatively little is known about the impact of undergraduate ambassadors, role models, mentors and tutors. In fact the biggest benefit of these schemes accrues to the HE students involved rather than the pupils. A study by Austin and Hatt (2005) suggests that the student am-bassadors improved their self-esteem and self-confidence, developed their transferable skills so that they could operate more effectively as learners and gained valuable experience to improve their position in the graduate labour market. And, of course, they can earn some money.

There has been a growing movement towards packages of a range of pre-entry activities, offering more sustained interventions with young people at different stages of their schooling. In England much of this activity takes place in Aimhigher and previously in the Excellence Challenge and Partnerships for Progression. Similar approaches can be seen in other countries, such as acti-vities organised by the regional forums in Scotland (Sinclair and McClements, 2004; Woodrow *et al*, 1998) and institutional strategies in Ireland (Osborne and Leith, 2000). Liverpool Hope University College has researched the impact of residential experiences for Year 9 and10 pupils with little or no HE family background (Atherton and Webster, 2003). Responses from parti-cipants indicate a large impact as a result of this intervention, with 84 per cent self-reporting that they are 'more likely to go onto HE'. Ninety one per cent of the respondents cited the project as 'quite' or 'very important' in reaching this decision. Further research at Liverpool Hope University College (2003) reports a limited and small-scale evaluation of a residential experience for 30 disabled students using student and staff questionnaires. In this study the majority of students indicated that being at Hope had made them 'more likely to come to university'. Similar results were obtained by Edmonds *et al* (2003) for students at a FE college, aged 16-30, with parents with low educational qualifications and non-professional occupations. However, there is no com-parison group for any of these studies and no follow-up to see whether these self-reports are converted into places in HE.

Research by Morris *et al* (2005a) sought to analyse the impact of Aimhigher: Excellence Challenge pre- and post-16 interventions on young peoples' aspirations to enter HE. The Excellence Challenge targeted young people mainly from households with no tradition of HE through attainment and aspiration raising activities and by providing financial incentives in the form of Opportunity Bursaries. Questionnaires were given to year 11 pupils, and given again in post-16 follow up. The responses indicate that successful tran-sition at 16 is more likely for those who took part in targeted educational interventions and who also had access to good careers education and guidance. The conclusions are tentative rather than definitive.

In a related study Morris *et al* (2005b) conducted a large-scale longitudinal evaluation involving young people, schools, further education colleges, higher education institutions and Aimhigher partnerships. Data was collected over two academic years from 19,998 Year 11 and 17,116 Year 9 pupils. Background characteristics at school and pupil level were controlled for and regression techniques were used to identify very small associations between policy interventions and pupil attainment. Similar evidence is presented by Emmerson *et al* (2005) in relation to Aimhigher: Excellence Challenge pre-16 interventions using comparisons between participating and comparator schools. Being part of the Aimhigher: Excellence Challenge programme was positively associated with attainment but did not increase the proportion intending to participate in HE in Year 9, although by Year 11 both attainment and aspirations had increased. Morris *et al*'s (2005b) analysis specifies which interventions at particular key stages had higher than expected impact on levels of attainment, including being identified as part of a targeted cohort, participating in summer schools and university visits and discussing higher education with university staff and students, friends and family.

Scottish research (Sinclair and McClements, 2004) tracked all students participating in the Lothians Equal Access Programme for Schools through to the first year in higher education. LEAPS is a widening access programme involving a range of partners and four HEIs. It is designed to increase the participation of pupils in HE whose opportunities have been limited by economic, social or cultural factors. It runs a range of activities to increase students' and parents' knowledge of HE, to provide impartial information about courses and HE routes, to raise aspirations about HE and to promote positive attitudes to learning and learning skills to facilitate the transition into HE. The research interviewed 928 pupils using the pre-entry application service. Of these students, 509 progressed to HE and 328 of these went to institutions in the region and could be tracked. The analysis found that no one factor had a statistically significant effect but that a number of factors might be significant in combination: previous qualifications, family background, summer school attendance and subject studied.

Hereward College, The National Integrated College for Disabled Students in Coventry, implemented and evaluated a widening participation project to facilitate disabled students, particularly those with complex learning support needs, to enter HE. The main thrust of the activities was to close the gap between further and higher education. They included partnership days, a summer school, and insight weeks, which were designed to bring disabled students into the higher education ethos and to make university staff more aware of the needs, opinions, hopes and fears of potential students with complex difficulties. Interviews with participants suggested that the programme was an effective way of increasing the numbers of disabled students who subsequently made successful applications to higher education from the college, with an increase of 300 per cent over a three-year period (Taylor, 2004). Again there is no control to show how specific this growth is.

Summary

Inequalities in educational participation are evident throughout the life course, reflecting multiple social disadvantages evident in initial education and affecting participation in later forms of learning. Parental income and education are particularly influential. Occupational status and family size are also relevant although the causal pathway is less clear. Quality of life factors (such as infant health) are important for understanding disengagement from education. The total proportion of the 16 year-old cohort remaining in education, government schemes, and employment-based training combined has remained constant for decades, even though the balance between the three routes has varied according to funding and availability over time. The majority of students in any study report wanted to remain in education to the next level. The decision to enter HE is often taken several years beforehand. The main reason for wanting to participate was to gain access to better employment. The main reported reason for leaving education was to begin earning a wage. Other reasons included not needing to achieve a level of qualification in order to pursue their chosen career, and the (non-explanatory) desire to stop studying and leave education. There is only limited evidence that not wanting to end up in debt was informing some young people's choice. The main predictor of whether or not pupils remain in education is success in their school examinations. Differences in aspiration between students from particular social classes were not evident, once differences in achievement have been allowed for.

Can patterns of non-participation be interrupted via educational and other interventions? Some pre-school schemes are generally beneficial although a causal relationship cannot be established, whereas others have little effect. But where the initiatives are beneficial in absolute terms they are not especially effective in reducing inequality. In some cases more advantaged students gain more, leading to an increase in inequality. There is limited evidence about the effectiveness of different pre-entry interventions with young people.

Much of the research in this area has focused on students' perceptions of interventions, rather than tracking them into HE. Students report that residential activities encourage them to attend HE. Where more in-depth research has been undertaken the evidence suggests that it is not possible to identify specific causes and effects of interventions. Woodrow *et al* (1998) and Woodrow *et al* (2002), in a series of widening participation case studies, find that institutions and WP partnerships generally have poor tracking data, and are often unable to assess the impact of their interventions. No single intervention to encourage school pupils to consider HE can be identified as making a substantial difference to actual patterns of participation.

7

The transition to higher education

This chapter summarises some of the evidence about the processes of application, admission and transition to HE, in the light of the earlier life determinants of participation discussed in Chapters Five and Six. It is important for readers to recall that from this point on, we are only discussing the selected group who do participate in HE.

Choosing an HE course

Lack of access to good advice and support has been suggested as a barrier for under-represented groups (Thomas *et al*, 2002). In general, prospectuses and visits/open days are rated the most helpful sources of information about HEIs, while IT-based media resources are the least helpful. Formal and informal advisers also play an influential role. Different applicants have access to and use different sources of information. Bowl (2001) found in her research with mature ethnic minority students on a pre-HE community based course that the students were disadvantaged in terms of advice and support from home and that this was not compensated for by official advice, support and guidance. Research carried out by UCAS (2002) found that while most students attended open days, GNVQ students were less likely to do so. These students were more influenced by their friends and families. There was evidence that the cost of travel deters some students from attending open days. This and the inflexible times were particular deterrents for mature and rural students. Connor *et al* (1999) found that mature students were more likely to have received visits from university representatives but overall used a narrower range of sources than younger (under 21) students, being less likely to use guides or careers fairs. Research and teaching quality assessments were used more widely by applicants from higher social classes.

Clearly a number of factors are involved in choosing an institution and a course and different students may prioritise different things. Reay *et al* (2001) note that geographical constraints such as the cost of living away from home and the costs incurred in commuting were present in working-class narratives of choice, but absent from those of the middle-class students. Non-traditional students, particularly mature and ethnic minority applicants placed more emphasis on reputation, quality, location and distance from home (Connor *et al,* 1999). Lack of access to local HE was identified as a barrier for students in rural and coastal areas in North Yorkshire, although traditional students did not show the same constraints (UCAS, 2002).

Awareness of their class meant that some young people applied to new universities rather than more élite institutions and for less prestigious courses (Forsyth and Furlong, 2003). Some working-class young people chose to do an HND or FE course rather than a full honours degree due to the extra cost of longer courses, particularly if their parents were unable to provide financial support. The exception to this was when students' overriding concern was to stay local. Other studies also indicate that many students had chosen institutions where they felt they would fit in. Leathwood and O'Connell (2003) and Read *et al* (2003) found that the non-traditional students in their research had chosen institutions where they felt they would not be different. For the mature students this was because they were fearful of being socially and academically inadequate compared with younger students. Those participating in this research had chosen a post-1992 institution because it was perceived as being friendly, less formal and more multi-cultural. Students from ethnic minority backgrounds feared that the lack of diversity in some institutions could make them feel isolated (see also Murphy, 2000).

Application and admissions procedures

Tables 7.1 and 7.2 show that across the UK home countries, social classes I and II predominate in HE because they predominate in applications for HE. These figures make it clear that the inequity in access to HE does not take place in the admissions process. Acceptances to HE (Table 7.2) are slightly more balanced in terms of social class than applications (Table 7.1). If anything, the admissions process favours classes IIIN-V. Again, the evidence suggests that the surface inequalities largely pre-date the HE transition process. Can anything be done, by this life stage, to overcome inequalities in the rates of admission?

Table 7.1: Applications to HE, UK 2001/02

	England	Wales	Scotland	N. Ireland	UK
I/II	52	53	55	42	52
IIIN-V	36	37	35	48	36
Not known	12	10	10	11	12

Source: Gorard (2005a)

Table 7.2: Accepted to HE, UK 2001/02

	England	Wales	Scotland	N. Ireland	UK
I/II	50	50	51	44	50
IIIN-V	35	37	35	46	36
Not known	15	13	15	10	15

Source: Gorard (2005a)

Clearly, such an aggregate analysis cannot take into account the nature of institutions, subjects and degree outcomes by social class or ethnicity. The entry requirements for different courses vary considerably and are closely related to the prestige and quality rankings of the institutions concerned (Abbot and Leslie, 2004). This can lead to social class differentials in specific subjects (Goddard, 2004). But the acceptance rates, even for subjects considered exclusive, were equivalent or better for the lower social classes. In this study applicants from both professional/managerial and routine occupational background had an 86 per cent chance of acceptance for Law, whereas students from a professional/managerial background had an 85 per cent chance of acceptance for Veterinary Science compared with 90 per cent for students from a routine occupational background.

A number of studies have analysed acceptance rates for ethnic minority applicants. Shiner and Modood (2002) found that applicants from ethnic minority groups (with the exception of Chinese applicants) had a lower rate of success in terms of initial and firm offers but were 1.5 to 2.5 times more likely to have been accepted via clearing and more likely to apply to a local university than white applicants. The authors note that in terms of A-level points the academic performance of applicants from ethnic minority groups meant that they were in a worse position to compete for university places.

The authors suggest that academic qualifications impact most upon success; the probability of successful application increased with improved A-level scores. Leslie *et al* (2002), using 1996-2000 UCAS data, suggest that there was no discrimination against ethnic minorities with A-levels; it was the lack of these qualifications that was the key to different acceptance rates. A smaller proportion of ethnic minority applicants were found to have two or more A-levels and overall A-level scores were lower than for whites although the reverse was true for Chinese applicants. In addition, a higher number of ethnic minority applicants had vocational qualifications.

Given these findings it is unlikely that compacts and special admissions arrangements could have much beneficial effect. Compacts are defined by the National Compact Scheme Project (2005) as

> The provision of opportunities for conferring some advantage in the admissions process (including the making of lower than standard offers) on individuals in disadvantaged circumstances or from disadvantaged backgrounds.

Special admissions arrangements and compacts in particular are used by just under 70 per cent of HEIs (Pennell *et al*, 2005). Despite the use of compacts to promote admissions to HE for students from non-traditional backgrounds, the National Compact Scheme Project found little evidence of their effectiveness. Few HEIs have data on the retention rates or on-course achievements of compact students.

The University of Glamorgan has operated a compact scheme for a number of years, which has been extended to include additional activities to assist transition and improve student retention. The scheme includes an introduction to university through 'Aiming for College Education' days, student tutoring, on-campus work-experience, master classes and study skills support. A points reduction for A-level students and a guaranteed place is offered to pupils who fulfil the compact criteria. Wakely and Saunders (2004) have undertaken tracking analysis of HE level 1 undergraduates who entered Glamorgan University through the compact scheme. The analysis compares 77 compact undergraduates with a matched pairs control group. The research aimed to address the issue of differential achievement at the end of level 1. There was no difference between the groups in terms of averaged module marks at the end of level 1. The study concludes that compact applicants have higher conversion rates than average, better retention rates and achieve a higher rate of direct progression to level 2 study. However, it is not clear that the lowest participation groups are being successfully recruited to the compact scheme in the first place.

Other studies are even less conclusive. Connelly and Chakrabarti (1999) found little evidence of the effectiveness of special schemes for students from ethnic minority backgrounds. Evidence involving semi-skilled and unskilled office and shop floor workers with no previous qualifications suggested that the courses were successful in recruiting a number of new learners, but the high rate of withdrawal shows that the course did not overcome all the barriers to learning (Loots *et al*, 1998). Reddy (2004), researching a Year 0 programme offered by an HE/FE collaboration to promote access to HE for mature students who had no NQF level 3 qualifications or their equivalent, also noted difficulties. The findings indicated high student satisfaction with the programme but poor rates of progression and achievement. Again, this suggests that despite a positive student experience, there are other barriers to HE access that must be overcome. It also highlights the danger of being mis-led by the majority of work in this field, none of which is based on a rigorous attempt at falsification, and most of which is small-scale and does not even use a comparison group when making claims of relative success. Hayes and King (1997) undertook a study into approaches to learning among students completing Access courses at nine further education colleges to investigate whether the courses prepare students for undergraduate study appropriately. They used an 'Approaches to Studying Inventory' questionnaire with the students to assess compatibility between their preparatory course and their HE learning. The findings suggest that Access courses might be inculcating attitudes, approaches and orientations to studying which are inconsistent with the majority of HE student experiences.

Foundation Degree programmes appear to be reasonably successful in attracting non-traditional learners; the majority in one study were mature, first generation students with alternative entry qualifications who were studying part-time (Dodgson and Whitham, 2004). Further research is needed to know the extent to which Foundation Degrees are attracting new learners who would not have accessed other provision had the Foundation Degree programme not been available. Watson (2002) reports a wide variation in the acceptance of non-traditional qualifications between institutions, with some institutions accepting less than 1 per cent of applicants with these qualifications to others accepting in excess of 70 per cent. Credit accumulation and transfer and the recognition of prior experiential learning (APEL) offer alternative routes into HE, particularly for mature students (Dunlop and Burtch, 2003). Such an approach requires compatibility between institutional programmes, full recognition of credit awarded by other institutions and overcoming negative views about students with non-standard entry qualifications.

The HE system is not obviously structured to provide compatibility between programmes such as between FE courses and HE provision or between HE providers to ease transfer from one institution or sector to another (Osborne, 2003). McGillivray and Knox (2003) examined institutional data for 1,794 students at the University of Paisley, considering entry qualifications and degree classifications. They found that 65 per cent of the graduate population but only 41 per cent of honours graduates used APL to enter into their programme at the university. Further investigation showed that a primary reason is because an honours route is not available to part-time students which affects many students using APL. The analysis showed that at honours level students with Highers or A-levels perform better than HND entrants but not better than HNC or other entrance qualifications. This suggests that admissions tutors can accept students with credit from various qualifications with few concerns about their ability to cope and gain an exit award.

There is relatively little research evaluating the impact of pre-entry interventions with adults. This is likely to reflect the current funding priorities in England, and Wales to a lesser extent, which focus on young people and the fact that many adult interventions are not targeted at access to HE but at engagement with learning opportunities more broadly. For example, Progression through Partnership is a project which aims to provide opportunities for people living in disadvantaged communities in south east Wales to progress from Level 2 to Level 3 qualifications and from Level 3 to Level 4 HE study. This is undertaken by delivering learning opportunities in community venues. People and Work Unit (2004) have evaluated the impact of the project in terms of widening participation and enabling progression to HE, sending a postal questionnaire to 45 per cent of the learners, 394 in total from which only 55 responses were received. This is an extremely poor response rate leading to considerable danger of misleading results. This limited data indicates that the project was successful in encouraging progression to HE, but as ever it reflects intentions to progress, rather than actual rates of transition. The research identified concern about the accuracy of targeting learners, because a large proportion of these learners already had higher level qualifications anyway.

The Action Learning in the Community project sought to explore innovative ways of widening participation via experiential learning, including some based in the community (Mayo, 2002). The study used an action research design, including evaluation, to examine the effectiveness of the project interventions in improving the employability of long-term unemployed participants. The research indicated that this modified approach succeeded in facilitating access to HE for disadvantaged adults as part of a holistic strategy, despite the disincentive of student fees and the lack of provision for financial maintenance. However, the research report contains no information about the size of the sample – which must cast doubt on its rigour. James and Preece (2002) undertook student tracking research to identify the common results and experiences of over 2,000 learners who attended a community delivered ICT course and who had childcare responsibilities. A high percentage of respondents went on to further study or paid employment, including 22 per cent who progressed to HE level study. A majority of respondents felt that the effects of the course were immediate, long-lasting or life-long and important. There is as usual no comparator group so we have no idea whether more or less than 22 per cent would have progressed anyway.

In summary, community-based interventions are claimed to be successful in reaching some adults who are able to progress to HE but the research data on progression is limited. Interestingly, many of these learners report wider benefits than HE progression. For example, Panesar (2003) researched the experiences of Asian women on targeted courses. The learners' testimonies illustrate some of the wider benefits of participating in learning: integration into the wider community, awareness of different cultures, adjusting to life in Britain, friendship, learning that others are in similar situations, drawing support from each other and empowerment through the skills and knowledge learnt.

The transition period

The transition to HE is frequently perceived as a fraught process for the majority of students but especially for non-traditional students. A common theme in many of the studies involving students from under-represented groups is learning to 'play the game'. For example, mature ethnic minority students in Bowl's (2001) research talked of the problem of understanding the rules of academia and tended to blame themselves when they failed to do so. Similarly, entrants from vocational routes who performed less well in HE compared to those with A-level qualifications took time to learn 'the rules of the game' (Hatt and Baxter, 2003, p18). Their previous educational experience had focused on developing skills that did not prepare them for the methods of assessment involved in academic HE programmes. In contrast, access course students and compact students involved in the research had participated in courses geared towards preparing students for entry to specific degree programmes. As a result these students had developed study skills, had regular contact with a liaison tutor and visited the HEI for lectures. The

A-level, access and franchise students were aware of the rules of the game in terms of assessment. Furthermore, they were more prepared for the social transition involved in the move to an HEI as a result of visits between staff and students and an existing informal peer support network. Students with vocational qualifications have to make both transitions: from vocational to academic programmes and from FE to HE. Evidence shows that mature students also experience difficulties making the transition to HE (Reay *et al*, 2002; Bamber and Tett, 2000, 2001).

Some young people report a lack of prior knowledge of what student life involves (Forsyth and Furlong, 2003). Consequently they were unprepared for the amount of free time they had and were unsure of how to manage this productively. Participants in the UCAS (2002) study expressed similar sentiments and felt they were under-prepared for the transition from 'cosseted learning style to mass independent HE' (p.30). Likewise, evidence of a lack of knowledge of the reality of student life was found in smaller studies of one post-1992 institution by Leathwood and O'Connell (2003) and another by Read *et al* (2003). Both found that non-traditional students, which included mature, first generation entrants and ethnic minority students, felt that they were expected to be too independent too early and were shocked by the lack of supervision and guidance. Further anxiety was created by not knowing what was expected in assignments, how to structure academic writing and about the standards of exams (Murphy and Fleming, 2000).

Drawing on an in-depth study of the experience of students with a disability, Hall and Tinklin (1998) suggest that locating parking places, specific offices and individuals and repeating requirements to different staff and departments all use up energy and time, leaving less of these resources to invest in social activities. This situation is exacerbated if the institution is not aware of individual student's needs prior to arrival. Students involved in the research had to undertake a process of negotiation with the institution to meet their individual needs. The difficulties experienced by disabled students can be compounded by physical restrictions which make it harder for them to meet people in the first important few weeks. The integration period can be more problematic for some disabled students (Hall and Tinklin, 1998) and this difficulty can continue beyond the transition period. Riddell *et al* (2004) identify the pressure of work and the lack of support as barriers to participation in social activity. Disabled students also experienced problems in identifying with the wider student body. This linked not only to the nature of their disability but also to other differences such as class and age. The authors emphasise the interaction between these factors and the institutional culture;

students who shared a similar cultural background to that of the institution found that other problems were reduced.

In relation to successful integration, students with a disability were also clear that they wanted a level playing field. They did not want to be singled out as different by academic staff or students or labelled as a 'problem' (Thomas *et al*, 2002). Students emphasised the importance of approachability and an open door policy, and found it daunting to challenge individual staff or departments (Riddell *et al*, 2004). Hall and Tinklin (1998) suggest that students with a disability received different treatment across different departments in the same institution. This is frequently linked to the personal experience of the staff involved rather than to any specific training (Kember *et al*, 2001). Indeed, it was felt that many academic staff wanted to help but were afraid of causing offence. Students' relationship to the department and the institution stems from and builds upon this initial relationship. Unfortunately, non-traditional students may be forced by their financial circumstances to move in and out of their studies so that staff have less time to develop relationships with them (Leathwood and O'Connell, 2003). This also affects their ability to become part of the student group and to participate in social activities.

Sanderson (2001) called for better support for disabled students in the transition from FE to HE and highlighted the need for better communication between the two sectors, clearer information for students delivered at the same time as information for non-disabled students and a named person or key contact for students within the institutions. This is also highlighted as good practice by Thomas *et al* (2002). Mentoring systems were identified as important in breaking down feelings of isolation and loneliness. Access to services and facilities was identified as a barrier by part-time students. Whilst full access and entitlement to services facilitates transition and integration, restricted access acts as a barrier (Kember *et al*, 2001). Perceived status also comes into play because part-time students do not feel valued as highly as full-time students if they do not have access to the same services.

Students who were unable to fit in with other students were in danger of becoming socially isolated, which could ultimately affect their confidence and commitment to their course. Kember *et al* (2001) also found that part-time and distance learners lacked both time and opportunity to meet fellow students. As a result their sense of cohesiveness as a cohort of students was reduced. Redmond (2003) reported similar findings with mature students who not only lacked the time and money to socialise, but felt conspicuous in places such as the Students' Union. Rhodes and Nevill (2004) found that men generally expressed more positive attitudes towards the factor 'access to university social life'.

Students who remain living in the family home, the majority of the participants in the study by Forsyth and Furlong (2003), experienced certain restrictions. The extra cost of travelling in terms of time and money limited how much they could become involved in social activities (Wilson, 1997). In addition, many worked part-time outside the university, further restricting the amount of time they had available. Holdsworth and Patiniotis (2004) highlight the difference in experience between home and halls students. Home students see university as an extension of college – just a change of bus route – and have little interest in university life beyond attending lectures. Those who seek to become involved find themselves trapped between the university, where they think they may not fit in, and their old community.

Working part-time outside the university led to some working-class students feeling that their identity was compromised and that they were more workers than students, which could lead to a loss of commitment and in some cases withdrawal. Many experienced an inverse snobbery and found the identity of being a worker more attractive. The work ethos was experienced more strongly by males, particularly those from disadvantaged communities. Negotiating conflicts of identity was also evident in research with mature students by Mercer and Saunders (2004) and Redmond (2003). The students, who were predominately women, felt that a lack of understanding created conflict between their home and university environments which led to feelings of isolation. To overcome this tension students strove to develop a dual identity, keeping the two halves separate or by seeking out those who understood their situation. This led to changes in social networks and the loss of old friendships.

Many non-traditional students report a lack of confidence in their ability to cope and experienced feelings of being at odds with the institution and with other students and staff (Wilson, 1997). This was particularly true of those students studying at élite institutions (Forsyth and Furlong, 2003). Even where there are higher numbers of non-traditional students within an institution, feelings of isolation are still evident due to the culture of the academy rather than of the student body. Factors such as the size of the institution, moving from building to building, and different formats for learning affect these students (Read *et al*, 2003). There may also be a tension between the concept of a traditional student as compared to a mature one (Reay *et al*, 2002; Holdsworth and Patiniotis, 2004). Becoming the traditional younger student means a combination of independence and dependence, leisure and academic work, which is alien to mature students. For them, becoming a student means sacrificing their social life and trying to satisfy competing domestic, academic and work demands. This can be particularly problematic for women.

Most of these issues relating to the transition of part-time, distance, mature or disabled students may not be barriers to participation so much as consequences to be faced by the HE system as a result of overcoming the barriers to participation for these students.

Summary
In the UK there are more applications for HE from students from social classes I and II, so these are over-represented in the take-up of HE. In terms of the threshold of entering HE or not (rather than allocating places at specific HEIs), the admissions process is at least neutral or even favouring those from less elevated backgrounds. However, applicants are faced by constraints that influence their choice of institution and course within HE. These include geographical constraints, cultural constraints, qualification level and type, and vocational relevance.

There is some lack of awareness amongst HE applicants of admissions practice, particularly in relation to the variance between published entry requirements and those that may be accepted later. Students entering HE have to learn to 'play the game', which is more of an adjustment for non-traditional students, particularly those entering with vocational qualifications. Disabled students may face particular limitations in relation to social participation. Many, especially mature, students report wanting a longer induction period offering a more supportive programme and providing a more comprehensive introduction to study requirements.

Access courses, Level 0 programmes and work-based learning routes, and access for students with no prior qualifications, offer some students opportunities to enter HE. Once in HE, these students do as well as peers who have entered via more traditional routes. Foundation degrees are successful in attracting non-traditional learners. However, it is not clear whether they are attracting new learners or those who would have accessed other types of HE provision anyway. Studies suggest that attendance at pre-entry summer schools enhances students' retention and success in higher education in the first year and beyond. Induction programmes can offer similar benefits to pre-entry summer schools in supporting students to make the transition into HE. What happens during the experience of HE itself?

8

Experiencing higher education

This chapter takes a brief look at the experiences of students once they are in HE, especially their learning experiences, and considers whether the structure and organisation of HE institutions could be a barrier to participation, progression or retention. It starts by considering patterns of retention and completion in HE before examining the possible causes of non-completion in more detail.

Retention and success

Overall, dropout from HE has remained at around 14 per cent for a decade, although Figure 8.1 on page 94 shows that the figures for dropout among Welsh students rose for two years, one before and one after the introduction of tuition fees in Wales.

Research on student retention and withdrawal identifies the significance of the institution in this process, rather than placing responsibility solely on the student (Dodgson and Bolam, 2002). Castles (2004) identifies support for students as a primary issue when considering the reasons for the withdrawal of part-time adult learners from the Open University. She states 'support figured highest of all in the analysis; mentioned by all interviewees' (p175). Further studies linking retention and student support include Warren (2003) and Murphy and Roopchand (2003). In a continuing professional development series about supporting student retention, Sellers and van der Velden (2003) identify 'targeted learning support' as one of the principles of retention. They argue that support should be targeted by being discipline-based, study skill-based, key skill-based and with pastoral support. Furthermore, support services and academic departments should work together to ensure that support is linked to students' study, particularly at critical junctures.

Figure 8.1: Welsh-domiciled students leaving HE institutions 1995/96 to 2002/03

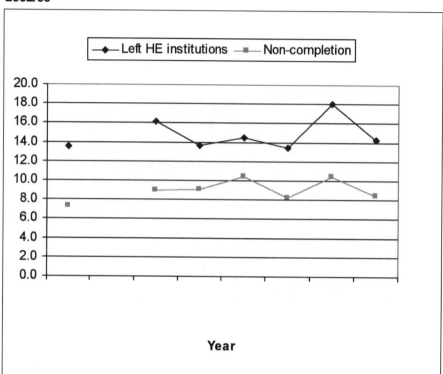

Source: HESA

Note: Non-completions do not include students who have officially completed their course or have transferred to another HE institution.

In a study of successful student diversity, Powney (2002) found evidence that institutions are moving towards providing support throughout a student's career in order to maximise retention. May and Bousted (2004) suggest that withdrawal was primarily due to lack of student support and unmet expectations. Lack of support from staff outside timetabled sessions and lack of peer support featured in the top fifteen issues cited as factors affecting students' decision to withdraw. They were reported to have experienced a high level of support prior to University and viewed support from staff to be an important aspect of their academic life. They expressed high expectations of the support they would receive and felt let down if it was lacking. Students who left in the first semester rated lack of academic support as a more important issue than students who stayed, indicating the importance of encouraging students to access support from the start.

Students are at increased risk of withdrawal in their first year of university, hence the need for targeted support (Roberts *et al*, 2003; Wallace, 2003). Chance (2004) instigated a project, targeted at first year students and addressing the theme of support, to act as an early warning system for the University to identify students at risk of withdrawal or non-completion. In Gutteridge (2001) the first six weeks are identified as the most difficult period for students due to financial and social resources being at their most limited and anxiety and expectations for social and academic integration being at their highest. In recognition of the importance of the first year, a project has been initiated at the University of Central Lancashire designed to improve retention rates amongst first year undergraduates with vocational qualifications (Jones and Abramson, 2003). The intervention incorporates a three-tier strategy: a residential summer school for those who received an offer, an elective first year module entitled 'effective learning' and a second elective module entitled 'mentoring effective learning' which is available in year two. The intervention is reported to have supported students' commitment to the university and the retention of under-represented students. However, as with all of the studies in this section, there is no serious evaluation of these claims.

Abrahamson and Jones (2004) assessed the impact of a three-day 'Flying Start' summer school for students entering the University of Central Lancashire with Advanced GNVQ qualifications as opposed to more traditional A-levels. The study involved the analysis of the academic records of over 500 students per year for three years, comparing the retention rates and achievements of this group with the rest of the student population. The analysis over a three-year period revealed that Flying Start students had a higher level of retention compared with the rest of the student population (Jones and Abramson, 2003). Research in Edinburgh also found that positive effects resulted from participation in a pre-entry summer school (Sinclair and McClements, 2004). An analysis of adult students entering the University of Glasgow via the Scottish Wider Access Programme (SWAP) revealed that SWAP students who had attended the Pre-University Summer School were more likely to pass examinations than other students (Walker, 1999). All these findings may be due to the nature of the students who volunteer to take part rather than the intervention itself and their claims require further validation by evaluations using control groups.

Additional examples of integrated support models are provided by staff at the University of Sussex (Morgan and Lister, 2004), Southampton Institute (Smith *et al*, 2005) and London Metropolitan University (Warren, 2003). Morgan and

Lister (2004) have developed a nine strand approach to induction which is aimed at improving the experience and retention rates of all students. The institution used national research and internal reviews to inform the development of the process. The authors claim that initial data shows an improvement in retention rates but few data are presented and the study is not yet complete. Smith *et al* (2005) report on the introduction of an institute-wide facility, namely Students 1st, which is aimed at providing 'an holistic, integrated and partnership approach to supporting student learning'. The component parts of Students 1st include a centrally located information centre, a student support network, a spiral induction programme and specific information, advice and guidance points. The facility is well advertised and used by students and is reported to have had a significant impact on student retention rates. The formulation of a new teaching and learning strategy underpins work at London Metropolitan University to enhance student re-tention (Warren, 2003). A team approach has been used with the goal of fortifying connections between teaching and student support and learning development. However, as with all of the studies above, there is no evidence of actual effectiveness or assessment of its overall efficiency.

More specifically, Castles (2004) identified two aspects that were particularly essential for a good personal tutor: availability and approachability. An in-formed, sympathetic and speedy response from a personal tutor was con-sidered to be necessary for students facing difficulties (Askham, 2004). Noble (2004) suggested that assistance needed to be accessible as early as possible to students who were thinking about dropping out. These findings suggest a need for greater awareness of Student Support Services (Dodgson and Bolam, 2002; Thomas *et al*, 2002).

Students may receive either support or antagonism and a lack of support from their family and friends. Either can impact on their higher education ex-perience. Generally, relatives were reported as being a major source of sup-port by students in reviewed papers (Borland and James, 1999; Higson *et al*, 2003; Riddell *et al*, 2004). But some students face pressure from the negative attitudes of family members and friends. For example, Bamber and Tett (2000) wrote that the working-class students participating in their project often felt a lack of entitlement to higher education (see also Chapter Seven). Living at home, although financially beneficial, can lead to being margina-lised from university life (Tett, 2004; Thomas, 2002). A number of ethnic minority students who were involved in research by Higson *et al* (2003) re-called that their parents had encouraged them to study locally and to live at home which led to them missing out on social events. Three quarters of the young working-class students involved in the project discussed by Noble (2004) lived at home for financial reasons. Half of them believed that this had impeded their ability to integrate socially at university. One example of responding to these problems is a University of Newcastle pilot Home Affiliation Scheme which supports students living at home by giving them access to the facilities available in halls of residence.

Life circumstances are more likely to push mature students into withdrawing from their course, compared with younger students, according to Ozga and Sukhnandan (1998) who concluded that older learners need greater institutional assistance to overcome external pressures, such as more flexibility in the duration of their course. Bamber and Tett (2000) noted that mature female students were more likely to talk about having to juggle home life and studying, whereas males were more able to separate their personal/domestic self from their academic life. Yorke (1999) also found differences between male and female respondents on full-time courses. Males were more likely to say that they had dropped out of university for financial reasons or because they had chosen the wrong course, whereas females talked of the demands of dependants and being unhappy with the social environment as influencing their decision to leave. This links to Dodgson and Whitham's (2004) finding that 36 per cent of Foundation Degree students had contemplated withdrawing from their course. The main reason given by these mature females was the pressure of working, studying and being responsible for a family, as well as returning to education after a long absence. However, Carney-Crompton and Tan (2002) found no difference in levels of anxiety between young and mature female students, even though the young women reported having a greater selection of individuals available for support.

Students from lower socio-economic backgrounds who took part in a Cooke et al (2004) study engaged in fewer non-academic activities such as sport clubs or societies and spent less time socialising than those classed as advantaged. This might be because these students were more likely than their advantaged peers to be in paid employment whilst studying. Part-time employment was a bigger influence on working-class students' decision to withdraw compared with those from middle or upper classes (Noble, 2004).

Overall, Roberts et al (2003) concluded that individual factors and career motivation played a greater part than support received or requested by students. Other authors also stress the importance of individual contextual factors (George et al, 2004, Bamber and Tett 2000, 2001). In summary what is found in different studies depends on the approach taken. The overall evidence-base is poor but it is unlikely that lack of support is the primary cause of student withdrawal.

Previous learning experiences

As suggested in Chapter Six, earlier educational experiences affect an individual's decision to participate in HE. They can also affect progress and retention (Donaldson and Graham, 1999). Students participating in a study by Castles (2004) portrayed a positive earlier educational experience as one of twelve factors contributing to student persistence in higher education. Problems arise when the new learning experience is not what was expected. For those who enjoyed initial education HE may be surprisingly different. For those who did not or who are participating after a break, it may be too similar to school.

There is evidence that students need to adjust to the teaching practices of higher education. Both Merrill (2001) and Richardson (2003) talk of students having mismatched expectations of the teaching and learning methods they will find in higher education. Despite taking different target groups of mature students and students entering from school, both studies found that student expectations were based on their experience of the formal and didactic teaching methods at school. Richardson describes the resentment of 750 students because the approaches they had been taught previously were no longer appropriate. On discovering that higher education was different from school, students had to learn how to become independent learners (Merrill, 2001).

The level of information provided in advance of a course was also reported to be a barrier for students. In a questionnaire study about the experience and perceptions of 94 first year undergraduates on a language programme (Chance, 2004), the adjustment to higher education was particularly problematic for students who had not received the right level of preparation before university. Similarly, some of the 608 students who responded to a questionnaire in Musselbrook's (2003) study accused the university of not providing enough information. Traditional students often express surprise on realising the proportion of self-learning and levels of self-motivation required at university (Cantwell and Scevak, 2004; Richardson, 2003). In HE there is a greater need to use published research and for students to analyse the material themselves (Rhodes *et al*, 2002). Those coming from vocational programmes additionally feel that they have insufficient experience of essay writing as opposed to reports, and of tests rather than larger assignments (see Chapter Seven).

Student motivation

The degree of motivation which students bring to their studies has been investigated as a potential determinant of the probability of completing their studies. Walker (1998) compared a group of students who withdrew from study with those who continued at university and found that the main differences lay in attitudes and motivation. She concluded that 'drop-out students were less motivated, less suited to academic work and had poorer attitudes' whilst 'successful students were highly motivated towards study'. In a study by Bennett (2003) motivation featured as one determinant of drop out but was not identified as important as either academic performance or the student's level of commitment to the programme. Sellers and van der Velden (2003) found that a number of students struggled with motivation, time management and organisation. In a review of research about retention for the Learning and Skills Development Agency, Martinez (2001) suggested that efforts to improve or maintain student motivation can lead to better retention and achievement amongst students.

In related research, Murphy and Roopchand (2003) used the Intrinsic Motivation towards Learning Questionnaire and the Rosenberg Global Self-Esteem Questionnaire with 160 students and the findings were analysed for different groups of students. Mature students were found to experience higher self-esteem and levels of intrinsic motivation compared with traditional students. Mature women were found to have the highest overall motivation and self-esteem scores. The authors speculate about whether mature students have developed a clearer perspective on the purpose of education, are more familiar with their preferences or make more informed educational decisions.

Teacher attitudes and perceptions can create barriers to effective widening participation, especially in relation to specific groups of students. Such barriers stem from staff assumptions about students in general or about specific student groups. When Clegg et al (2003) investigated motivational problems among first year undergraduate students through interviews with teaching staff, the issue was posed as a 'student problem'. Motivation was also presented as an 'Asian problem' as their discussions of motivation were 'overlaid by a racialising discourse' in which Asian undergraduate students were blamed for having poor motivation. Staff in Taylor and Bedford's (2004) study focused on student-based factors as the reason for withdrawal rather than identifying teaching practice and curriculum design as factors. Following a study of the experiences of 32 mature, non-traditional students as they make the transition to higher education, Bowl (2001) questions the tendency to see students from non-traditional backgrounds as a problem, rather than scrutinising the educational institutions who are responsible for their progress. Students with disabilities may also be perceived from a 'deficit' perspective. For example, the study by Fuller et al (2004) identified staff attitudes to be a factor in determining whether these students' needs were accommodated by the institution. We review research on the experience of students with disabilities later in this chapter.

Could the apparent link between motivation and drop out as assessed after students have dropped out be an illusion created by the research itself? Obviously, those who drop out of HE will report being less motivated to continue than those who stay on but this does not mean that lack of motivation is the cause of the drop out. Bad experiences in HE are only some of the reasons given for withdrawal (Harrison, 2006). Different aspirations and lifestyles do not necessarily mean low aspirations (Watts and Bridges, 2006). One reason why removing barriers may not work, as discussed in Chapter Six, is that the theory of motivation is invalid (Ahl, 2006). Not wishing to continue studying or preferring to pursue other activities may not be a problem, and so does not need any explanatory theory of motivational deficit. Ahl (2006) suggests that the idea of lack of motivation is usually a problem for someone other than the prospective student, and can even represent an unwarranted exercise of power over that person's lifestyle.

Assessment and feedback

Varying assessment practice emerged in Richardson and Woodley's (2003) study of indicators of performance. They used HESA data to investigate the role of variables such as age, gender, subject studied and mode of study as predictors of attainment for students awarded degrees by higher education institutions in the UK. They found variations in academic attainment between different groups of students which were partly determined by the different teaching and assessment practices encountered in different academic disciplines. More specifically, case study research by Powney (2002) looking into widening participation learning and teaching practices, draws attention to the differing efforts made by universities to use alternative means of assessment for students with disabilities, enabling them to demonstrate their skills and knowledge as effectively as possible. Powney states:

> what emerges clearly from the case studies is how adjusting methods of learning, teaching and assessment to meet the needs of a very wide range of students – including mature students and disabled students – in practice benefits all students (p5)

This research demonstrates the value of an integrated approach to assessment, which is less focused on the outcome and more on making assessment integral to the learning process. Another common factor was to encourage students to reflect on their own learning George *et al* (2004) go as far as to argue that self-assessment is a vehicle for mainstreaming students from disadvantaged backgrounds. In several studies authors provide evidence that changes to assessment practice towards the greater involvement of the student in the assessment process, has had a positive impact upon students' perceptions of assessment (Povey and Angier, 2004; Peasgood, 2004; Noble *et al*, 2003).

Merrill's (2001) study of the perceptions of adult learners found that students had contradictory views about types of assessment. Some expressed a preference for examinations, as they were less time consuming than assignments, whilst others expressed a strong dislike of examinations. Students are reported to have altered their perceptions towards assessment over the course of their studies, especially with respect to learning 'how to cope with the university system' (George *et al*, 2004; Peasgood, 2004; Povey and Angier, 2004). McAuley (2004) asked 397 students to indicate the perceived importance of different methods of assessment (individual, group, dissertation, examinations, presentations and peer assessment) and their satisfaction with these methods. Students rated the importance of an assessment method greater than their level of satisfaction with the method. Satisfaction levels were higher for individual assessment and examinations which are traditional methods whereas group work, presentations and peer assessment showed higher levels of dissatisfaction overall. Both McAuley (2004) and Merrill (2001) demonstrate that student attitudes towards different methods of assessment vary, and that these variations demonstrate that students do not always prefer more innovative methods of assessment.

The importance of student opinions about their assessment experiences is a central message in studies considering assessment (James, 2001; McAuley, 2004). In Fuller *et al*'s (2004) study a high number of students reported experiencing difficulty with assessment methods in relation to their disability, including coursework (34%), examinations (30%) and presentations (12%). Similarly, in Hall and Healey's study (2004) students reported having problems with assessment methods as a result of their disability, particularly with written examinations and coursework. Assessment caused the respondents greatest problems, with between 37 per cent and 63 per cent of students reporting difficulties. But Riddell *et al* (2004) report that staff felt that adjustments to teaching and learning would 'lower standards' and give an 'unfair advantage' to disabled students (p23).

The experience of students with disabilities

There are conflicting opinion as to the need and desirability of targeting policy for disabled students more generally. Avramidis and Skidmore (2004) argue that this would be counterproductive to a move towards inclusion. Powney (2002) notes the tension which exists between an inclusive approach to teaching and learning and recent changes in higher education, such as increasing the student:staff ratio or reducing the time staff spend with students. Hall and Healey (2004) argue that devising general policies to support the teaching, learning and assessment of disabled students may not always meet the specific needs of individuals. There is also a problem of implementation. Riddell *et al* (2004) found that universities were reportedly committed to identifying the needs of disabled students but that this was not matched by a willingness to adapt their teaching and assessment practice.

It is notable that studies focusing on the barriers experienced by students in different teaching contexts particularly involve students with disabilities. The predominant teaching context which is most problematic for disabled students was lectures. In the study by Hall and Healey (2004), 46 per cent of 80 disabled students from six universities indicated that they had faced barriers to learning in lectures. Examples of barriers include the number of slides presented, the lack of a break, the speed of delivery and the difficulties of listening or watching and note taking. Similar findings were reported in a survey of 173 students (Fuller *et al*, 2004), where 44 per cent of them reported having problems in lectures which were associated with their disability. Examples included the lecturer talking too quickly, removing display material too fast, and trouble with their own note taking. There were additional barriers in other teaching contexts for disabled students, including during fieldwork which required them to make notes in the field and independent work involving research for an assignment or dissertation, where 40 per cent of 80 students reported problems (Hall and Healey, 2004). In the study by Fuller *et al* (2004), 12 per cent of 173 students reported difficulties in similar off-campus contexts such as fieldwork and school placements. Technology and digital media can both overcome and create new barriers (Beacham and Alty, 2004). Apostoli (2005) highlights the barriers to participation for dyslexic students in the inaccessibility of teaching materials.

Getting students to declare their disability if it is not visible is essential so that they can be provided with the required support. This was found to be difficult by Dodgson and Bolam (2002) and Thomas *et al* (2002). This means that individuals may start higher education without their support systems in place, giving them a negative introduction to university life. Students with

mental health problems or with dyslexia suffered in this way, often only receiving an assessment of their needs when their situation became overwhelming.

Most of these studies made no attempt to contrast these findings with those
from students without disabilities who may also find speed of delivery, lecturers removing slides too quickly and other factors to be important barriers
to their learning.

The need for institutional change

Is institutional change needed to attract and retain students from different
under-represented groups and in universities, colleges, the FE sector and
community-based HE? If the culture or institution of HE changes to accommodate diverse students, there is no research evidence on the impact that
this will have on students from traditional backgrounds, who currently remain the majority of students. This is equivalent to the ethical dilemma discussed in Gorard (2002d). Will the benefits of HE as outlined in Chapter Nine
still hold under these changed circumstances?

From an institutional perspective Foskett (2002) discusses whether widening
participation is simply a marketing challenge to reach those who have never
considered post-compulsory learning or a cultural challenge. He suggests
that it 'is inherently a challenge to internal institutional culture that requires
colleges to change fundamentally their *modus operandi*, their view of the
world and their values'. Bowl (2001) reports that the institutional context
remains unresponsive to the needs of students from non-traditional groups
and that this impacts negatively on the experiences of mature ethnic minority
students. Similarly, Longden (2000) finds resistance to institutional change in
the HE sector which generally wants to retain élite instincts and traditions.
Thus there are inherent tensions between HE policy and the aspirations of
the sector. Evidence that institutional change is required if students from
non-traditional backgrounds are to thrive in HE is also presented in Layer *et
al* (2002).

This need for institutional change, especially in relation to mature students,
is supported by research by Ozga and Sukhnandan (1998) on student withdrawal. Research with mature working-class males also concludes that
universities need to change if they are to offer an image and environment that
will appeal to these types of students (Marks, 2000). Foskett (2002) finds that
widening participation is firmly established at the strategic level in the FE
sector but it has not impacted on the culture of institutions, due mainly to the

project-based nature of much widening participation activity and to limited awareness of the complexity of the needs and wants of current non-participants.

The culture, ethos and values of the institution can either repel or encourage students from under-represented groups and indirectly hinder or support their success (Thomas, 2002). Atherton and Webster (2003) use case study evidence to argue that institutional change, as well as individual, family and community change, is necessary to enhance the retention of students from under-represented groups, a point supported by Bamber *et al* (1997). Read *et al* (2003) argue that students from non-traditional backgrounds are disadvantaged by an institutional culture that places them as 'others'. For example, the typical student is often assumed to be young, and with no other responsibilities. This influences policies, practices and projections about HE. Flexible timetabling or childcare facilities are special requirements and not the norm.

Timetabling needs to match both students' needs and their other commitments. Mature students would find it easier if they received their timetables earlier in the year to give them time to organise childcare and employment (Dodgson and Bolam, 2002). Bamber and Tett (1998) found that inflexible course arrangements disadvantage adults with domestic responsibilities. Even in post-1992 institutions with a commitment to supporting widening participation there remains a focus on full-time continuous study and have little opportunity to switch to part-time and tend to leave rather than change their mode of study. Similarly, ethnic minority students may not want to attend institutions where they are an isolated minority and working-class students report being put off applying to certain institutions which they feel are snobbish (Read *et al*, 2003). Pickerden (2002) shows how part-time, community-based provision can meet the needs of Muslim community groups, particularly women. However, there is still no evidence about the benefits of part-time studying for students from under-represented groups. Woodrow *et al* (2002) found little evidence that part-time provision attracts young students from lower socio-economic groups into HE.

Summary
Students motivation to learn is related to their personal values and aspirations and the material rewards for completing the course. Motivation appears to affect student retention and withdrawal and therefore efforts to improve or maintain student motivation can lead to better retention and achievement. However, the evidence on this is in danger of being tautological. There is

slight evidence that teaching approaches are being adapted for diverse learners, despite recognition in the literature that particular target groups, such as mature learners, have specific needs. There is, however, a tendency for non-traditional students to be perceived by teachers from a 'deficit' perspective, for which compensatory approaches have been offered. Some research questions the appropriateness of the higher education curriculum for an increasingly diverse student population. Some HEIs separate students from non-traditional backgrounds to provide generic skills instruction to bring them up to the standard of others. There is no evidence as to whether this is an appropriate thing to do. Finally, there is little evidence of universities adapting their assessment methods to cater for the diverse educational backgrounds of students; rather the emphasis is on the students learning to adapt in higher education. Varying the forms of assessment seems to benefit all students, not just those from particular target groups.

Between 1994/5 and 1998/9 student numbers in England increased by 18 per cent, but income only rose by 7 per cent during the same period. This was mainly through additional sources of income rather than planned public expenditure (UUK, 2001). This overall decline in funding per student has been accompanied by changing patterns of student demand which together have caused a majority of institutions to operate below the 3 per cent retained surplus recommended by the funding councils (Watson, 2002). Longden (2000) uses comparative data to demonstrate that the UK spends less than other high income countries on higher education. A small study by Boxall *et al* (2002) found that the costs of widening participation are significant and not spread evenly across the sector. There is no evidence about the extent to which the increased widening participation premium has relieved this problem but it is likely that institutions with high numbers of widening participation students have lower units of resource per student, rather than higher, as the evidence would suggest is required.

These financial pressures on HEIs set the context in which policies to attract, support and retain non-traditional students have evolved. Lack of support has been mentioned as an influential factor in students' decisions to withdraw from university courses, while the existence of support for students has been claimed to contribute to their successful completion of degree programmes. The first year is often targeted, as this is when the majority of students withdraw. Some students associate personal tutors with general problem solving, particularly students who do not live at home, rather than with the more positive role of guiding the learning process. Student Services are becoming more centralised and proactive in an attempt to reach students in need. However, better collaboration between support and academic staff is needed to prevent students from slipping through the net. Academics often have a poor understanding of the function of Student Services and frequently do not refer students, and students are uncertain about what kind of support is provided. Students may be reluctant to initiate links with support services because of the stigma involved, particularly with mental health services.

Conclusion

9

Graduation and beyond

The focus of this book is widening participation in HE, and the barriers to participation that potential or marginal students may encounter. What happens to HE students thereafter, in terms of postgraduate opportunities for further study or employment may therefore seem irrelevant. But it is important to consider this before deciding whether what has happened to students after HE in the past could be a barrier for future students. This chapter considers patterns of postgraduate participation in HE and the labour market returns to HE for non-traditional students.

Access to postgraduate study

Increases in participation in undergraduate HE have been accompanied by greater numbers of graduates entering postgraduate study to pursue their academic or career aspirations. In particular, there has been a dramatic increase in the numbers of students studying at Masters level (Hoad, 2001). A study by HEFCE (2005) found that around a fifth of young entrants who qualify with a first degree also study at postgraduate level, giving an estimated young postgraduate participation rate of 4 per cent. The rise in this participation rate may reflect a need for giving a clearer signal to employers, as undergraduate participation rates have increased. Keep and Mayhew (2004, p309) comment that 'those from higher socio-economic groups have ways of fighting back, through acquiring additional human capital (for instance, via Masters degrees)'. Sloane and O'Leary (2004) estimate that a higher degree provides an hourly earning boost of 114 per cent for a man compared to a similar man with no qualifications, while the comparable figure for a woman is 132 per cent. Smith *et al* (2000) found that a graduate's class of degree, degree subject, prior qualifications and social class not only affected their success in the labour market, but also influenced the probability of their undertaking further study. More recently, HEFCE (2005) found that for first degree qualifiers the participation rate for most types of postgraduate study varied little according to the background of the entrant. However, qualifiers from disadvantaged areas were nearly twice as likely to progress to post-graduate teaching courses. Overall, given the disproportionate number of those from advantaged backgrounds amongst degree qualifiers, the tradi-tional-age participation rate of those from disadvantaged areas is 1.4 per cent compared with 6.6 per cent for advantaged areas. This is a similar degree of inequality to the rate of young undergraduate participation.

Barriers to widening participation in postgraduate study

Potential barriers to accessing postgraduate study were identified by the National Postgraduate Committee (NPC) (Hoad, 2001) and include:

- Access to financial support

- Childcare needs

- Inappropriate or inflexible timetables

- Access to facilities outside undergraduate teaching times

- Pressure from employers

- Age-related problems

- Perception that postgraduate study is only for a particular type of academic person

In Australia Wakeling (2003) researched the link between social class and pro-gression to postgraduate study on completion of a first degree and found that 'centrally collected data are patchy, but where available suggest that the undergraduate pattern of class inequality continues at postgraduate level'. In addition, graduates from pre-1992 universities are more likely to study for a PhD regardless of social class. If participation in postgraduate education re-flected the composition of the population, 25 per cent of students would be from lower socio-economic groups. In reality the figure is around 10 per cent (10.4% in 1997). Education is the most popular subject area (approximately 15%) while Law has the lowest proportion (6%).

The data is even more limited about the participation and experience of post-graduate students with disabilities. Croucher *et al* (2005) found that graduates with disabilities were slightly more likely to progress to further study than non-disabled peers. Anderson (1995) interviewed 28 postgraduate students studying taught programmes and for research degrees in Australia. She found some differences between the barriers faced by men and women with disabilities. In particular, men were more encouraged to study at post-graduate level than women. Women faced additional problems such as divisions between domestic labour and study, finding uninterrupted time and space to study and lack of support from rehabilitation providers. They faced battles with compensation boards and with social security for women returning to study, as well as having perceptions of unusual treatment by academics because of their disability. Anderson *et al* (1998) note that some of these barriers will be faced by all women but they are likely to be more acute for some disabled women.

Finance has been identified by some in the UK as a barrier to accessing post-graduate education and successful completion. The Higher Education White Paper 2004 did not address the needs of taught postgraduates. In particular, postgraduate students not only have to pay higher fees than for under-graduate education but they are not eligible for any financial support on the basis of income. Fees for taught postgraduate courses are typically triple the current undergraduate level and there are few studentships (Wakeling, 2003).

In Australia an analysis of 1993 and 1995 enrolment data in postgraduate courses, which were taught programmes as opposed to research, found that the introduction of the Higher Education Contribution Scheme (HECS, incor-porating fees for postgraduate courses) had a negative impact on disadvan-taged groups' access to postgraduate study. A further study was undertaken in 1998 to extend this work to examine the evidence of the impact of the intro-duction of tuition fees on enrolments in taught postgraduate programmes in Australia (Anderson *et al*, 1998). The study involved a statistical analysis of stu-dents enrolled in taught programmes in 1993, 1995, 1996 and 1997 by target group. By definition this analysis excluded the students who may be worst affected by financial barriers to participation in postgraduate courses – those who were not participating. But this shortcoming was ameliorated by the in-clusion of questionnaires and interviews with final year undergraduates and students who had graduated three to ten years before, and interviews with staff. These studies found that female students from lower socio-economic groups and students from rural families were significantly deterred by finan-cial barriers. Students from non-English speaking backgrounds were not de-terred by the costs any more than any other group and had a proportionately slightly higher rate of enrolment than in undergraduate HE. Students of indigenous backgrounds were enrolled in taught postgraduate programmes at a rate equivalent to their participation in undergraduate education. There was insufficient data about disabled students to reach any firm conclusions. The studies found that the financial barriers to participation in postgraduate study are the direct cost of study and a reluctance to accumulate further debt when they already had debts from their undergraduate study.

There is a greater tendency for ethnic minority degree graduates to enter postgraduate education than white graduates. This trend is particularly strong amongst Chinese and most Asian groups, as opposed to black graduates (Connor *et al*, 2004). Black Caribbean and black other graduates are more likely to pursue vocational than academic routes through postgraduate study. In summary, access to postgraduate study is unlikely to be a significant barrier to undergraduate participation.

Estimating labour market returns to HE

Widening participation research in Britain and elsewhere has largely neglected the possibility that the postgraduate labour market may itself act as a barrier. This neglect itself reflects the overwhelming evidence from the 1970s up to the present that graduates receive a significant earnings premium when compared with non-graduates, and the assumption that these relatively high economic returns are and will continue to be available to all qualified entrants to HE. There are also limitations in the datasets available for the analysis. For these and other methodological issues, see Gorard *et al* (2006). Since the 1960s a large number of earnings function studies have found high average rates of return to graduation in the UK compared with alternative ways of investing the costs involved. Recent studies (Chevalier and Walker, 2001; Dearden *et al*, 2002; McIntosh, 2004; Blundell *et al*, 2005) confirm these findings and suggest a higher rate for female graduates. On average, therefore, traditional UK entrants into HE do face economic incentives. So the labour market should generally act as an attraction rather than a barrier, although some commentators dispute the economic returns from learning (Wolf, 2002), with the National Child Development Study figures (see Chapter Two) suggesting very little impact of qualification on earnings (Wolf *et al*, 2006). What about the evidence for non-traditional students?

The results of recent UK research provide data for an initial examination of the extent to which the labour market provides economic incentives for non-traditional students to enter HE. Certain groups of potential entrants may receive systematically smaller earnings premiums after graduation and hence receive lower rates of returns than the average. In such a situation these groups would have no economic incentives to participate in HE and, to the extent that this occurs and is known about, the labour market could be a barrier to widening participation. Anticipated economic rewards to HE study take the form of its normally positive impact on life-long employment, reflected in higher earnings, social status, other non-pecuniary benefits and lower incidence and duration of unemployment. The dominant approach to investigating these benefits has been through micro-econometric studies which typically concentrate upon a very narrow measure of benefits, though social mobility research has also explored the determinants of the occupational attainment of graduates.

Recent studies suggest different economic returns by entry qualifications, social class, degree class, subject area and HEI. For example, Johnes and McNabb (2004) find that students from poorer backgrounds are more likely than others to drop out of university. Smith and Naylor (2001) find that social class has a strong effect on degree performance and Smith *et al* (2000) reports that graduates from poorer backgrounds have a lower probability of being employed in graduate occupations. Blasko (2002), based on a relatively small sample four years after graduation, also found that male and female graduates from lower socio-economic backgrounds received lower salaries than graduates from more advantaged backgrounds, and were less likely to be in graduate jobs. In addition male, but not female, graduates from working-class backgrounds were more likely to be unemployed as were black male graduates and male graduates of Bangladeshi, Indian and Pakistani origins. The same study found that older male graduates received lower salaries and were also disadvantaged in terms of the level of their post-graduation jobs. However, Asian women, but not the men, earned less than their white graduate counterparts.

McGuinness (2003), surveying a Northern Ireland cohort, concludes that for any pre-entry qualification, subject choice and degree classifications are more important determinants of rates of return than the quality of the university attended. Naylor and Smith (2004) analyse HESA data for the entire population of 1998 leavers to provide more detailed analysis of degree performance. In pre-1992 universities they find significant negative ethnic origin effects for all but female Chinese students. For example, Indian students have an approximately 10 per cent lower probability of obtaining a good degree than white students. Naylor and Smith (2004) also found that some reported disabilities have significant negative links to degree performance. Dyslexia is associated with a 6 per cent lower probability of obtaining a good degree for male students. However, whilst all disabilities have negative coefficients, the low sample size for specific disabilities prevented the researchers from drawing more detailed conclusions.

In combination these findings raise the possibility that some marginal entrants to HE face rates of return which are insufficient to provide financial incentives for HE participation. This is largely due to their differences in completion rates. An additional and related concern is that that the recent rapid expansion of HE in the UK has increased the inflow of graduates into the labour market at a faster rate than the creation of new graduate-level jobs and lowered the earnings premiums of new graduates. This is known as the 'over-education' phenomenon. If this impacts disproportionately on certain groups with low overall participation rates in HE it may also represent a barrier to widening participation.

The 'marginal learner'

Dearden *et al* (2004b) use the 1970 British Cohort Study to identify the wage returns from staying on in post-compulsory schooling and completing HE for variously defined marginal learners when they were aged 29-30 in 1999/2000. The acknowledged limitations caused by low sample sizes, the possible selectivity of the non-responding groups and the omitted variable bias suggest that this innovative approach should be viewed as an exploratory analysis. The authors find that there are substantial returns both from staying on and completing HE for all sub-groups of the population defined by socio-economic background, family income and ability, with more variation amongst males and higher returns for females. For staying on after compulsory schooling the study found, subject to data limitations, that individuals from poorer families who drop out would have enjoyed substantial returns from staying on (around 13% for men and 17% for women). Returns from the attainment of any form of HE, conditional on having achieved at least level 2 qualifications, were generally higher than for staying on after compulsory schooling. Overall those with intermediate probabilities of achieving HE experienced significantly higher returns from HE than those with either higher or lower probabilities. Thus, as Dearden *et al* (2004b) point out, if marginal learners are defined as those on the cusp between going to HE or not, they generally face significant financial incentives to enter HE. For men the returns from HE are substantially higher for the disadvantaged groups (low social class, low income family and low-ability) than for advantaged groups. In contrast to men, women were found to have similar returns from HE across, ability, income and social class groups.

In this sample the marginal learners were making their HE participation decisions in 1989. The rapid expansion of HE since that date has altered the average returns from HE study (Adnett and Slack, 2007) and it is likely that the profile of the marginal learner has also changed. In addition, by focusing on average returns for specific sub-groups the degree of risk and uncertainty attached to those education returns are neglected. This may be an important factor for less well-off families. Finally, since men are more likely to be working full-time in their early 30s than women, there are problems with making gender comparisons.

Indirect barriers to success in the labour market exist for students from educationally disadvantaged backgrounds. Employers systematically favour graduates with certain educational characteristics: good A-levels, high status HEIs, specific degree subjects (Pitcher and Purcell, 1998) and a good degree classification (Purcell and Hogarth, 1999). Brown and Hesketh (2003) report that one organisation received 14,000 applications for 428 vacancies. Graduates from Oxford University had a one in eight chance of success, while applicants from new universities had a one in 235 chance, although the researchers had not used a control group to look for other differences. Chevalier and Conlon (2003) use cohorts of graduates from 1985, 1990 and 1995 to explore the impact of institution type on returns in the labour market. They found evidence that more prestigious institutions, especially Russell Group HEIs, provided higher financial returns to their graduates compared with other institutions, particularly post-1992 institutions. Whilst their findings are far from robust, confirmation of such a premium would reinforce social and cultural divisions in the labour market, as the Russell Group and other pre-1992 institutions attract fewer students from non-traditional and educationally disadvantaged backgrounds and the majority of working-class students attend post-1992 institutions (Keep and Mayhew, 2004; Leathwood, 2004).

The literature therefore suggests that graduates from non-traditional backgrounds do less well in the labour market, even when other variables such as entry qualifications, institution attended, subject studied and degree classification are adjusted in the statistical model (Hogarth *et al*, 1997). Lower socio-economic groups receive lower salaries than graduates from more advantaged social backgrounds and are less likely to feel that they are in graduate positions (Blasko, 2002). Working-class male graduates experience more disadvantage in the labour market, such as periods of unemployment, and are less likely to be in managerial or professional posts than their middle-class counterparts.

Graduates from lower socio-economic groups

Widening access to higher education has done little to boost the chances of working-class graduates joining the professional elite. These graduates are improving their position in the labour market but are not securing the top jobs with the highest salaries or with the most prestigious employers (Brown and Hesketh, 2003).

There appear to be both direct and indirect barriers to success in the labour market for graduates from lower socio-economic groups. For example, Caspi *et al* (1998) find that personal and family characteristics begin to shape labour market outcomes years before people enter the labour market and these remain significant even when educational duration and qualifications are taken into account. In their qualitative research Purcell *et al* (2002) find that many employers do not believe that social class is a significant variable in graduate recruitment. However, the researchers conclude that discrimination is implicit as competency-based recruitment favours those with the confidence that middle-class cultural capital endows. For example, they found that 'most of the assessment centres that we examined included structured events that allowed self-confident and articulate candidates to shine' (p15). In contrast Bond and Saunders (1999) conclude that poorer returns from the labour market are largely to do with individual ability and motivation. They find that class background and parental support are significant but much weaker than these other factors.

Hills' research in one HEI suggests that non-traditional students either do not know where to look for information for their job search or that they were not using it (Hills, 2003). She also presents some evidence suggesting that working-class students can disqualify themselves from particular professions as they believe that they will not fit in or that they will not be recruited. This may be due to lack of self-confidence or to having a caricature idea of some employment fields. Personal and family characteristics also relate to indirect negative effects in the labour market, primarily linked to educational choices. For example, some of the reasons why graduates from lower socio-economic groups do less well in the labour market are related to the institutions they attend, the subjects they study, the class of degree they obtain and their HE entry qualifications (Blasko, 2002). This may be compounded by the fact that students who are the first in their family to enter higher education are less likely to relocate from their domicile region to attend an HEI (Belfield and Morris, 1999), which restricts their choice of institutions. They are also less willing to relocate to find graduate employment, which is associated with higher status employment (Dolton and Silles, 2001). Blasko (2002) found that students from lower socio-economic groups are less likely to participate in extra-curricular activities that contribute to CV-building and better opportunities in the labour market.

Ethnic minority graduates

In general, ethnic minority graduates do less well in the labour market, at least initially, than white graduates (Bailey, 2003; Shiner and Modood, 2002; Hogarth *et al*, 1997). They experience more difficulty in securing a job after graduation and are more likely to be unemployed (Connor *et al*, 2004; Blasko, 2002). However, rates of unemployment vary between different ethnic minority groups and are mediated by gender. Studies generally find that ethnic minority men are more likely to be unemployed than ethnic minority women but it is not clear which groups of males are most likely to be unemployed. According to Blasko (2002) it is most likely to be Black, Indian, Pakistani and Bangladeshi men, while Connor *et al* (2004) identify Pakistani and Chinese men as particularly disadvantaged. The situation relating to Chinese men is ambiguous. Connor *et al* (2004) use 2001/2 HESA data to demonstrate that Chinese graduates are more likely to be unemployed, while Blasko (2002) also uses HESA data but argues that Chinese graduates are less likely to be unemployed. Unfortunately, Blasko (2002) does not present the data needed to verify this claim.

Once ethnic minorities have secured employment, the evidence indicates that they do well. Blasko (2002) finds that ethnic minority graduates are no less likely than other graduates to be in a graduate job and Connor *et al* (2004) tentatively conclude that they are on average in better jobs than white graduates. This positive conclusion is tempered by evidence from Battu *et al* (2000), which suggests that ethnic minority students are more likely to be over-educated for their employment than whites, where over-education is defined as being 'employed in jobs for which their current qualifications are not required'. Bailey's (2003) survey has sample sizes that are too small to verify or question the claim by Battu *et al* (2000).

Ethnic minorities, particularly black graduates as opposed to Indian and Chinese graduates, are under-represented in the graduate intakes of large firms (Connor *et al*, 2004). This could be a consequence of discriminatory recruitment procedures which cause indirect discrimination, such as recruiting on the basis of A-level scores, using competency frameworks, tests or assessments that are biased against different cultural and education backgrounds and interview bias. Large and prestigious employers tend to favour particular institutions, which are usually pre-1992 institutions with high average A-level entry scores and a strong academic reputation. These institutions have smaller numbers of ethnic minority students, with the exception of Chinese students (Shiner and Modood, 2002). Indirect discrimination is reinforced by the low expectations about the labour market held by some minority students and the low expectations of HE staff who direct them to less challenging careers (Hills, 2003). Both Connor *et al* (2004) and Hills (2003) identify the lack of ethnic minority role models, especially at middle and senior management levels, as contributing to the low expectations of students and their advisors. But the efficacy of providing such models is far from established.

Leslie and Lindley (2001) find that language ability contributes to non-white disadvantage in the labour market experience, but when language effects are removed non-white males still have higher rates of unemployment and lower earnings. Hills (2003) identifies dialect and discrimination as linked. In her study, HE staff report that some ethnic minority students speak a fusion language, not just with friends, but in the university, and that they are likely to use this in interviews and not do as well as their more traditional peers in securing high status employment.

Mature graduates

There is some evidence indicating that mature graduates find the transition into the labour market harder than younger graduates (Conlon, 2001). Smith *et al* (2000) find that men aged over 33 are six percentage points more likely to be unemployed or inactive than men aged less than 24 at graduation, while women between 24 and 33 are at least two percentage points more likely to be unemployed or inactive than their younger peers. Entering HE after the age of 24 has negative labour market effects for male and female graduates, including increased risk of unemployment, poor career prospects and less likelihood of achieving a graduate level job (Blasko, 2002). Egerton and Parry (2001) found that the rates of financial return for mature graduate women were only 5-6 per cent compared with those who did not enter higher education. For mature graduate men it was only about 1 per cent. Egerton and Parry (2001) estimate that with the additional costs of higher education, tuition fees and loans rather than grants to cover living costs, new mature male graduates could make a sizeable overall loss from participating in HE. Purcell *et al* (2002) found that the number of new graduates over the age of 30 who were recent recruits to traditional high flyer jobs was very small. Such recruits were more frequently found in difficult to fill vacancies.

There is limited evidence about why mature graduates experience disadvantage in the labour market. In one London institution some employers reported that they preferred younger graduates, particularly in some fields such as law (Hills, 2003). It is also likely that mature graduates are less able to relocate to find higher status employment, which can have a negative impact on job opportunities (Dolton and Silles, 2001). In Purcell *et al*'s (2002) study it was widely argued by employers that mature students de-select themselves from fast-track programmes on the grounds that they are more likely to have dependants, less likely to be geographically mobile and less willing to undertake the kinds of activities (frequent travel, long and unpredictable working hours and/or moves within the UK or abroad) expected as part of such programmes. This raises the question of whether such requirements are essentially core aspects of these high flyer vacancies in organisations that build them into graduate training programmes.

Disabled graduates

There is surprisingly little research about disabled graduates and the labour market. Hogarth *et al* (1997) find that disabled graduates have lower earnings than non-disabled graduates. Research by the Disabilities Task Group of the Association of Graduate Careers Advisory Services (AGCAS) specifically looked at the destinations of 2003 graduates with disabilities self-declared whilst in HE compared with non-disabled peers, by analysing HESA first destinations data for full-time graduates (Croucher *et al*, 2005). Unlike other research, this study examined the experiences of disabled graduates from specific groups: with dyslexia and unseen disabilities, blind and partially sighted, deaf and hearing impaired, wheel chair users and mobility difficulties and mental health issues. This study found that graduates with disabilities do slightly worse in the labour market compared with their non-disabled peers but they are more likely to progress to further studies. However, the difference is less pronounced for those with unseen disabilities.

Conclusion

The stratification of the undergraduate student body described in Chapter Three applies also to postgraduate study.

It is tempting to conclude from the results of microeconometric studies of earnings functions that the labour market is not currently a major barrier to widening HE participation. There are significant economic rewards for marginal entrants to HE suggesting that there are potentially net social benefits from dismantling the barriers preventing the exploitation of these gains.

However, the nature of the data analysed in the studies above means that the total number of observations available for many of the narrowly defined under-represented groups in HE are too few to yield reliable comparisons. These sample size limitations means that previous research provides little information about the incentives provided by the UK labour market for HE study amongst most ethnic minorities, the disabled and late entrants.

Larger databases and well-targeted and constructed micro studies are needed before we can fully assess whether the labour market represents a significant barrier to widening participation for certain minority groups. However, even if these were available and it was concluded that the labour market was a barrier for low participation groups, the cause of this barrier would still need to be investigated. Hence the importance of research which explores the matching process in the graduate labour market, looking at both graduates' employment search patterns and graduate employers' search be-haviour.

10

Overcoming the barriers to participation

I n this final section of the book we specify gaps in research and areas where more research is needed before there can be general agreement among commentators and policy makers. We make more general observations about HE research and summarise areas in which there is strong evidence or on which there is already general agreement. We continue with a discussion of the nature and purpose of HE and conclude by re-visiting barriers to access.

Some implications for research

In reviewing the literature for this book we found problems in the nature and use of existing large-scale datasets. It is not clear what the problem addressed by WP actually is nor whether it is getting better or worse over time. There are no ideal datasets for the analysis of patterns of participation in higher education in terms of policy levers, or social, economic, and regional disparities. All existing datasets suffer from one or more defects: they include only participants, have incomplete coverage, have substantial proportions of missing data or cases, have changed key definitions over time or are incompatible in range or aggregation with other datasets. These and other difficulties lead analysts to focus mainly on young participants taking their first degree and this may bias public and so policy perception of HE issues. One of the key constraints when analysing rates of participation is the availability of data that provides an accurate baseline or population figure with which to compare the number of students.

Given these methodological constraints we propose two areas of development. First, greater consideration should be given to the research, both policy-oriented and academic, potential of data collected by HESA. For example, this may mean that there is greater consultation on the form and nature of datasets that serve all stakeholders' interests. Secondly, there need to be better links between school data and HE data. This could be in the form of a unique pupil identifier as now used in compulsory education or a look-up table available to researchers that would directly link individual pupils to individual HE and FE students. If this is not possible then alternative links could be made between school data and HE data. For example, HESA records the previous secondary school attended for students attending HE institutions. However, this data has been given low priority by HESA in its collection and quality assurance. This variable could provide a very useful way of tracking individuals, or small groups of individuals to very local areas. Rates of participation could then be considered by previous education establishment, enabling better targeting of resources in the encouragement of greater participation in HE.

We also found problems in identifying high quality relevant research evidence. Of around 60 per cent of relevant pieces encountered that actually presented evidence, of which only a subset gave sufficient information to make some judgement of quality, a high proportion showed substantial flaws. Other than weakness in reporting evidence, the most common generic defect was the link between the evidence presented and the conclusions drawn from it. A number of problems kept resurfacing, including lack of controlled interventions to test what works, lack of suitable comparators even in correlational and observational designs and the exclusion from the research of those not participating in education even in research about non-participation. A typical piece of work in this field involves a small number of interviews with a group of current participants in HE, often from the same institution as the researcher. Such a study cannot uncover a causal model, is difficult to generalise from and tells us nothing about non-participants, the group that much work in this field is ostensibly concerned with. There is no agreement about how to compare differences over time and place. There is a general abuse of the purpose of statistical tests of significance. These flaws are so common and are not specific to research concerning widening participation in education. So they are not generally remarked on by authors, picked up in peer-review nor taken into account when attempting to draw warranted conclusions from one or more studies.

It is important for readers to be aware of the limitations of the existing evidence on widening participation. Traditional narrative literature reviews are often uncritical while even in a standard 'systematic' review the limitations of research are not clear for the simple reason that most research is routinely excluded from the review, either because it is not a randomised controlled trial or because it is not of high quality, either in the conduct of the research or its reporting. If we had adopted a similar approach there would have been almost nothing to discuss. We encountered no randomised controlled trials, nor trials of any kind. Many pieces of research were reported inadequately and many were of poor quality. Instead of simply excluding nearly everything we decided to summarise what there was, but to ensure that readers are aware of the limitations of our approach.

Using HE research as an example, a more general lesson can be drawn for lifelong education, and for those who research it. When considering the impact of measures to improve education, such as initiatives to remove barriers to participation, there is an ethical responsibility for all evaluators to be appropriately sceptical. The scale or tenacity of the impact must dwarf the bias introduced by measurement errors, missing cases and changes in data collection methods over time. There is no technical answer to the decision on how large or sustained the impact must be. It has to be convincing in context and with caveats to sceptical observers (Gorard, 2006a). Only then is it ethically appropriate to use public funding to act on the conclusions of the research (Gorard, 2002d). The topics of most themes in this book could be subjected to rigorous trials if the authors claiming that they know what works in removing barriers to participation were prepared to test their claims by scientific scrutiny.

To demonstrate impact it is important for the evaluation to be conducted independently of the WP programme, partly because funding for WP programmes, and therefore the jobs of those involved, is often dependent upon success, thus creating the potential for bias. It is common for a programme to consider only those involved, expose them to some experience of HE and then report that the participants had thought more about HE after the event than before it. This is not a surprise. It is equally important that the evaluation is set up from the outset with clear objectives and pre-specified success and failure criteria. Putting money and energy into a new programme must have an impact of some kind. So that finding some kind of impact after spending time and effort on a programme is not a surprise and is far from concluding that the programme achieved what it set out to do. The evaluation must include a 'fair test' of the programme such as a randomised controlled trial or similar. It is absurd to compare the perceptions of a group of volunteers attending a residential experience of HE with the perceptions of those who did not volunteer, yet this is the kind of comparison that is found in the literature.

A considerable proportion of our review considered the impact of interventions intended to widen participation and our conclusion was that no interventions can be identified which make substantive differences to patterns of participation in HE. There are a variety of reasons for this. Most importantly, a majority of interventions made no attempt to test or demonstrate impact in terms of participation. A few studies looked at patterns of application but not at success or subsequent participation. Sometimes an evaluation of impact was attached to the programme *post hoc* and sometimes the evaluation was in terms of how programme participants reported that they felt. Mostly there was no comparison with either a control group not receiving the intervention or with the situation before the intervention. Non-participants in school, college or HE were routinely excluded from studies attempting to understand or ameliorate non-participation in school, college or HE. We found no attempt to measure the economic efficiency of the programmes.

Some interventions were not yet mature and this represents a major intractable problem for impact evidence. Our review of evidence took a life-long view of the trajectory towards participation or otherwise in HE and it was clear from this view that many of the most important determinants of participation appear early in life. It is possible to predict with disconcerting accuracy which individuals will end up in HE, and which will not, based solely on what is known about them at birth. Relevant factors include sex, ethnicity, first language, parental education and occupation and place of birth. The addition of determinants from early life and compulsory schooling increase the accuracy of predictions substantially. Qualifications and route at age 16 and subsequent life events make less difference, because often a learner identity has already been formed with a subjective opportunity structure that either includes or excludes HE. To be fully effective, interventions need to occur early in life. Interventions in post-16 participation and in the process of application and admission to HE face a greater challenge to make headway in changing the subjective opportunity structure of an individual. However, interventions in earlier life which have been set up in the last decade are too recent for the participants to be old enough to enter HE. Even when enough time has elapsed it would be scientifically misleading to attribute an outcome to an intervention which took place so long ago and with so many intervening variables.

In summary, we know little about the following fundamental questions concerning WP:

- True contextualised patterns of participation – who actually gets what in HE? The quality of datasets makes it hard to say who is currently being 'excluded' from HE, who ought to be participating and how this is changing over time. This also makes it difficult to judge the success of large-scale attempts to widen participation

- What actually works, cost-efficiently among smaller-scale interventions to widen participation? Those advocating specific interventions often claim success for them, but most interventions have had no rigorous evaluation. We encountered no randomised controlled trials or similar. This makes it difficult to judge the success of any attempts to widen participation in the short term

- Part-time students, finance and motivation. Existing datasets make it easier to focus on full-time students. This may be causing bias both in research and, even more importantly, in policy making

- Non-participants are largely ignored in the research literature, excluded both from education and also from the research intended to address their exclusion

- Early life factors. When precisely does the gap in educational equity appear and why? Even life-course studies are left with an absence of causal model. How are the correlated factors such as poverty linked to educational opportunity?

- We found little research about the trends, experiences, barriers and interventions faced by disabled graduates. This is a significant omission in the context of the funding council's policy commitment to widening the participation of disabled students

- Another neglected area is the experience of students who withdraw part way through their HE course and enter the labour market. Does a brief HE experience accrue labour market advantages or is it a disadvantage when seeking employment?

- Of the target groups used throughout the review, those classed as 'looked after children', whose support needs and support systems are likely to differ from traditional students, are not addressed.

Summary of evidenced conclusions

Our analysis has shown some indications of discrepancies in HE participation by social groups and geographical areas. However, rates of participation are equalising over time, the introduction of different methods of financing have not disturbed long-term patterns, there is almost no drop out due to lack of finance and the qualified age participation rate is near 100 per cent. Financial barriers to access have received increased attention with the introduction of variable fees. However, the returns available to the marginal learner from the labour market still suggest that HE is a sound economic investment. This is supported by research from Australia that has found that the introduction of a student contribution scheme to cover the costs of HE has not altered participation in HE by students from lower income groups. Furthermore, when HE was free to students and living costs were covered by a grant, participation in HE by social class was not more proportional or more equitable than it is now.

There is a danger that the widening participation debate is hijacked by fees and finance issues at the expense of more far-reaching institutional, life-long and societal change. There is no evidence of large scale inequity in HE admissions. Social classes are currently represented in HE in reasonable proportion to their prior qualifications. There may well be unfairness in the admissions procedures for some institutions or departments but this is not reflected in the overall figures. The problem does not lie with the proportion of applications turned into admissions but with the numbers and types of applications themselves. What then are the implications?

The widening participation agenda is in danger of addressing the wrong issue. Through misunderstanding of the numbers involved some policy makers and evidence providers have combined to try to solve a problem that does not exist. The dominant policy interpretation of the determinants of participation is in terms of the individual's calculation of the net economic benefits to be derived from education and training, as proposed within human capital theory (Becker, 1975). This is what leads to the plausible sounding metaphor of barriers. But the reality is more complex (Gambetta, 1987; Fevre et al, 1999). The opportunity cost of this misdirected effort is that the problems that do exist remain unsolved. We could use the resources saved to address the issue of why the discrepancy in prior qualifications occurs.

We have little knowledge of what works in trying to widen participation to those not participating and least likely to participate, rather than the usual

suspects (Macleod, 2003). There are different definitions of widening participation informing different aspects of government policy and interventions:

- an access discourse, focusing on raising the aspirations of a few gifted
  and talented working-class students to enter the top institutions

- a utilitarian discourse focusing on getting more people into HE to
  serve the needs of the economy by providing pre-entry support,
  supplementary study skills and vocationally relevant programmes

- transformative discourse of widening participation through broader
  engagement and institutional change.

A more explicit understanding of widening participation is required. This is
likely to include who is to be targeted, whose responsibility it is, whether all
institutions should play the same role, and whether it is national policies,
institutions or individuals that must change.

Students from non-traditional backgrounds are often portrayed as in deficit,
and therefore in need of additional and separate provision to rectify perceived weaknesses. This is evident in discussions of student support where
separate support is provided for particular groups of students rather than
support being made available for all students. The research reviewed illustrates how staff often perceive problems such as withdrawal by students from
under-represented groups as the fault of students, but further analysis finds
shortcomings in learning, teaching, support and institutional issues. This
suggests that institutional change is required for support to become em-
bedded in the institution. But a key tension is between making special provision for non-traditional students and marking them out as deficient in
some way. Much of the research takes the structure of the current HE system
for granted and focuses on relatively minor changes to improve the opportunities and experiences of students from under-represented groups. The
growth of the part-time sector, mature entry, non-traditional prior qualifications and the conversion of polytechnics and colleges into universities
reflect considerable change in the HE sector in England and Wales in the last
decade. But this transformation has not matched the scale of change from an
élite to a mass system in terms of student numbers. Entry to HE is mostly on
the basis of traditional means, programmes are largely unchanged, full-time
study is the norm, leaving and re-entering HE is comparatively difficult and
effective credit transfer is elusive.

This brings into sharp focus a key question about the nature and purpose of
higher education. In widening participation to currently under-represented

groups are we seeking to offer a pre-existing experience of HE more widely or are we expecting to change the nature of HE to accommodate the new kinds of students? Christie *et al* (2005) describe how non-traditional students attend high prestige universities on a local day basis for pragmatic and financial reasons. Previously, attendance at a high prestige university was on a boarding basis. In fact, many Oxbridge students find little difference between university and the culture of sixth-form boarding in private schools. The increase in day students means that the prestigious HEIs are widening participation by changing the way in which students experience HE. The WP day students report missing out on social and information networks which are available to traditional boarding students. This is a small example but it shows clearly that the first option of retaining a traditional HE sector open to access by 50 per cent of the young age group plus mature students over the age of 30 may not be possible without a level of funding based on a higher proportion of GDP. Widening participation has and will change the HE sector, including the experience of the students. It is already pertinent to ask whether a foundation degree student in a college of HE is experiencing anything like the same thing as a student taking an honours degree in a high prestige university. But changing the nature of HE as experienced by WP students calls into question the purported advantages of HE for the individual, society and the economy which are predicated on past experiences. There is currently a tension between a perceived economic imperative and an inclusive definition of a learning society, which may end up in conflict.

Another question inevitably raised by our summary of evidence concerns the element of compulsion now attached to post-16 education and training, including HE (Tight, 1998). As participation widens we are faced not so much with a learning divide where opportunities are only available to some as with individual learning choices. Many people obtain much of their adult education through private reading, informal sources such as friends and cultural institutions such as museums and art galleries (Lowe, 1970; Gorard *et al,* 1999c; European Commission, 2001). At one level informal learning is simply learning 'which we undertake individually or collectively, on our own without externally imposed criteria or the presence of an institutionally authorised instructor' (Livingstone, 2000, p493). Informal learning is clearly valuable but because it 'is not typically classroom based or highly structured, and control of learning rests primarily in the hands of the learner' (Marsick and Watkins, 1990, p12), this means that it is not susceptible to targeting or even measurement in the same way as FE and HE.

The education system in England and Wales has compulsory schooling for all, based loosely on a comprehensive and egalitarian model until age 16. A greater element of selection is introduced to continuation at 16+, such that prior attainment begins to influence how and even whether an individual continues in formal education and training. This is despite growing pressure for everyone to continue formal education in some way. Some individuals leave formal learning at or even before 16 and never return. On one reading of the evidence this is a key target group for the widening participation agenda: those least likely to participate again. But those least likely to participate again are largely ignored as poor bets in favour of those more like the usual suspects for HE. Most of £2 billion intended to improve literacy and number skills for adults in the Skills for Life programme was actually used for 16-18 year-olds who were already enrolled on college courses (Clancy, 2005). Unsurprisingly, this enormous expenditure led to no overall improvement in adult literacy over four years. At age 18 individuals face a heavily selective HE system in terms of prior attainment, with little semblance of comprehensiveness. At best only 50 per cent of the population will be offered this learning experience. It is this abrupt change and the anomalies it produces that lie at the base of the WP issue.

To reach the conclusion that more WP work needs to be done to ensure equity for low income students 'requires the joint assumptions that innate ability to benefit from education is completely independent of socio-economic circumstances and that equality of opportunity is essentially perfect for school education' (Hutton, 2005, p4). Neither has had much evidence presented for it. One possible set of explanations for the current under-representation of particular groups in HE rests on merit. There is the possibility that at least some of these surface inequalities are more equitable in Rawlsian terms than they seem (Rawls, 1971). If prior attainment is a key determinant of entry to HE, and qualifications are generally deserved by the individuals concerned, then there is no injustice and no especial need to widen rather than simply increase participation. One reading of equity such as that proposed by Rawls says that surface inequalities are only inequitable if they are not based on 'talent', where talent includes ability, motivation, and diligence.

Bond and Saunders (1999) warn against a thoughtless assumption that individuals from less advantaged socio-economic backgrounds fare worse in education and later life because of their class position rather than their prior ability or ambition. These authors present an argument, using the National Child Development Study data (NCDS, 1958, see Chapter Two), that the biggest influence on later occupational achievement for any individual is their ability, as measured by cognitive tests. Next most important is their motivation, as measured psychometrically. Once these are taken into account, then class origin is almost irrelevant as an explanation. These conclusions are not popular and have been as much disputed, as have their obverse which is the idea that all individuals start as a blank slate. Nevertheless there is a high correlation between the results of cognitive ability tests and later social class and between social class and qualification and between qualification and HE participation.

Using a similar approach, Nettle (2003) shows that childhood ability is associated with adult class mobility in a way that is uniform across the social classes of individual origin. This suggests that there is a high level of meritocracy in the UK and little evidence that individuals from less privileged backgrounds have to be more talented to succeed than those from privileged ones. In addition, although this is not the point made by their authors, one of the most notable features of the transmission matrices produced by Blanden *et al* (2005) from both NCDS 1958 and BCS 1970 is the high level of social mobility in the UK for both cohorts. In both cohorts, around 17 per cent of those born to the poorest families end up in the richest quadrant and vice versa. If there were no financial inheritance and perfect mobility then the maximum this figure could be is 25 per cent. The difference from the ideal of perfect mobility in these tables containing 2,000 cases is represented by only about 25 cases in each of the wrong extreme cells.

The measurement of ability and the idea of a relatively stable motivation have both been heavily criticised. The idea of IQ as an innate general cognitive ability is now largely abandoned within psychology (Nash, 2005), making deficit theories used to justify unequal opportunities less plausible and certainly less widely accepted. We now have multiple intelligences, a revival of Dewey's collective intelligence and an attempted separation of potential as in the potential to learn language but which requires exposure, skill, and ability in terms of the capacity to carry out skilled actions. This is another example of the difficulties of drawing warranted conclusions over time, even from cohort studies. The meaning and acceptance of variables measured in one era, such as psychometric data from the 1960s, are no longer seen as valid in a later era. We could still compare IQs over time but may no longer wish to do so.

Perhaps, instead, we should devote resources to reducing inequity in sixth-form retention and attainment, or in compulsory schooling. Perhaps we should spend our widening access funds at the pre-school level (Feinstein, 2003), or on reducing poverty and disadvantage more directly. Education is probably an inefficient, and certainly a very slow, form of social engineering. Given that it is possible to predict with alarming accuracy the qualifications of individuals at age 16 and their chances of staying on in education simply from what is known about them at birth (Gorard, 1997) we need to direct our resources more towards families and wider society. By the time they are 16-18 years-old many non-participants did not include the possibility of further or higher education in their 'subjective opportunity structure' (Gorard and Rees, 2002). As we have seen, they also tended not to have traditional entry qualifications. They were not aware that they had a choice of whether to participate in HE or not. Consequently they did not report being deterred by the costs of HE, or of unfairness in the selection process. They may not have been tempted by financial incentives.

Paradoxically, as participation in HE increases it may lead to greater polarisation between the majority of individuals who are able and willing to attend HE and a decreasing minority forever excluded. The question has to be asked: if we work to increase the currently under-represented groups then who is meant to be left out (Watson, 2004)? If no more places are funded in total, as is happening in England, then every new WP student must displace someone else. Who? Perhaps what we should do instead is to use the widening participation agenda and the political willingness to deal with at least one part of the Cinderella sector that is adult education and the funding that flows from it, to address the much more widespread inequalities that really do exist in adult and continuing education. In summary, if nearly everyone who is already qualified to attend university chooses to do so, then we need to create greater equity of access qualifications. This can be done at school and is probably already being addressed by school policies. What we can also do is to use the fashionable enthusiasm for widening participation to make changes to adult and compensatory education where a real improvement is possible at relatively little cost.

We urgently need high quality evidence of what works to widen participation, particularly to consider the impact of pre-entry interventions with adults. The current funding priorities in England and the available high quality datasets focus on full-time students and the participation of young people. Alternative entry routes to HE in Sweden, intended to help the most under-represented, actually advantaged upper middle-class men the most and so increased class bias in HE (Berggren, 2007). Many adult interventions are not targeted at access to HE but at engagement with learning opportunities in general. Even these tend to fail. For example, plans to create a new entitlement to stepping stone courses for those with few qualifications have apparently been damaged by funding rules in England (Lee, 2006b).

This book demonstrates that patterns of participation in higher education are highly influenced by family background and early experiences. Disrupting the non-participating trajectories is a larger task than the higher education sector can cope with. However, widening participation policy and practice needs to address not just access to HE, which has been the focus of much national and institutional policy making in recent years, but the experience these students have in higher education too. Without addressing the nature of the higher education sector there is a danger that we will continue to perpetuate inequality, with certain students only having access to certain types of higher education experience such as Foundation Degrees or being more likely to withdraw early from HE.

There is a potential paradox in the widening participation agenda. If qualifications are deserved and used as entry requirements for HE then it would be inequitable to change the system so that it is easier for less deserving others to get places. Rawls' (1971) difference principle would point out that it would be inequitable for someone with talent who has worked hard at school and home throughout their childhood to have the same chances of reward as someone with less talent who has not worked hard. Equally, if an individual's level of qualification is not deserved then it is unfair to use this as an entry requirement for HE at all. We should either accommodate the applicant, or act so as to bring them to the required entry standard. We are in a position as a society where we say that public examination results mean something, are a recognition of talent and can be used to decide on future life events. It is legal for employers to use them as a discriminator in selecting applicants for jobs, for example. On the other hand, at the same time we say that these qualifications are unfairly distributed across social groups and so are not deserved. We should either abolish the use of qualifications as a discriminator or seek political remedies for the non-educational inequalities that preordain educational inequalities.

In a study which compares students entering higher education with academic and vocational qualifications, Hatt and Baxter (2003) found that a vocational background helped students develop a set of skills that did not prepare them for the assessment regime they encountered on an academic course of study. Their assessment results were found to be lower until they learned the rules of the game. Other studies focusing on prior educational qualifications, including Hoskins and Newstead (1997) and Rahidzab et al (1999), address the link between qualifications and performance. These studies consider variable entry qualifications and question whether they are a useful indicator of performance. They find that the type of qualification students entered with was only a weak predictor of subsequent performance. They argue that the results offer clarification that opening access to students with non-traditional qualifications has not led to any diminution of standards. Smith and Gorard (2007) also demonstrate the futility of attempting the equivalent of a school-effectiveness study in the HE sector where the outcome measures are not standardised or moderated. This lack of standardisation means that degree results, for example, are almost inversely related to intake qualifications such as A-level grades.

Older applicants and applicants to some HEIs such as the Open University do not require traditional entry qualifications. In many ways this is also an anomaly producing confusion for WP. Given that estimates of the qualified age participation rate are currently near 100 per cent, a more consistent policy of only allowing qualified individuals into HE would mean that fewer people would participate as adults and then mostly when they had later attained the level 3 qualification that they did not have at age 18-19. WP would then consist of two major strands: improving the equity of the school system and making it easier for older adults to return to formal learning whenever they wish (Harvey and Slaughter, 2007). Neither approach is currently being used. The school system is diversifying and therefore segregating students by socio-economic status. Funded opportunities for adults to take part in learning are being reduced.

A more consistent policy of abolishing the need for prior qualifications and the system of selection in terms of qualifications would overcome the inverse ageism of the current system and transform the HE sector. It would truly *widen* in addition to increasing access. Perhaps discrimination by qualification will soon seem as unnatural as discrimination by sex, class, ethnicity, sexuality, disability and age do now. All of these were once considered acceptable (Walford, 2004). There is a high correlation between level 3 qualification and university success and between university outcome and success in employment but we must be cautious about what this signifies. The correlations exist largely because we create them. Students are only encouraged to stay at school if their GCSEs are good, only accepted at university if their level 3 qualifications are good, and are more likely to be offered a good job if they have a good degree from a good university. Level 3 qualifications are highly predictable from earlier attainment, life events and personal characteristics (Gorard, 1997). Taking a life course view, qualifications are not causing subsequent success in education but act as a substitute variable, summing up the prior individual, social and economic determinants of success at school and beyond (Gorard and Rees, 2002). We do not select potential HE students on the basis of socio-economic status, ethnicity, age or disability, as this is both unfair and illegal. However, we do select them on the basis of a substitute variable that sums up and is heavily correlated with such background factors. Why? The current approach is clearly not engineering a truly inclusive route to HE qualification.

References

Abbot, A. and Leslie, D. (2004) Recent trends in higher education applications and acceptances, *Education Economics*, 12, 1, 67-86

Abramson, M. and Jones, P. (2004), 'Empowering Under-represented Students to Succeed in Higher Education', in D. Saunders *et al* (eds.), *Learning Transformations: Changing Learners, Organisations and Communities,* London: Forum for the Advancement of Continuing Education, 347-353

Abroms, L. and Goldscheider, F. (2002) More work for mother: how spouses, cohabiting partners and relatives affect the hours mothers work, *Journal of Family and Economic Issues*, 23, 2, 147-166

Action on Access (2005a) *Making a difference: the impact of Aimhigher. Work with communities and outreach activities*, www.actionaccess.org

Action on Access (2005b) *Making a difference: the impact of Aimhigher. Mentoring, ambassadors and student associates*, www.actionaccess.org

Action on Access (2005c) *Making a difference: the impact of Aimhigher. Progression to higher education from vocational, work-based and work-related learning*, www.actionaccess.org

Action on Access (2005d) *Making a difference: the impact of Aimhigher. Work with specific widening participation target groups*, www.actionaccess.org

Adnett, N. and Slack, K. (2007) Are there economic incentives for non-traditional students to enter HE? The labour market as a barrier to widening participation, *Higher Education Quarterly*, 61,1, 23-36

Ahl, H. (2006) Motivation in adult education: a problem solver or a euphemism for direction and control?, *International Journal of Lifelong Education*, 25, 4, 385-405

Ahmad, F. (2001) Modern traditions? British Muslim women and academic achievement, *Gender and Education*, 13, 2, 137-152

Anderson, D., Johnson, R. and Milligan, B. with Stephanou, A. (1998) *Access to postgraduate courses: Opportunities and obstacles*, Higher Education Council. Canberra: Australian Government Publishing Service

Anderson, E. (1995) *Issues and Barriers in Postgraduate Education for People Who Have a Disability,* A report for the DEET Cooperative Project, Victoria. Auspiced by Deakin University and Victoria University of Technology

Apostoli, G. (2005) Developing 'content' in a creative curriculum that is flexible and engaging for new learners, in A. Ackland, J. Samuel, D. Saunders and J. Storan (eds.) *Access, Retention and Employability: Transforming Higher Education*, FACE

Archer, L. (2000) *Social class and access to higher education*, Report of the Social Class and Widening Participation to HE Project: University of North London

Archer, L. (2002) Change, culture and tradition: British Muslim girls talk about Muslim girls' post-16 'choices', *Race Ethnicity and Education*, 5, 4, 359-376

Archer, L. and Yamashita, H. (2003) 'Knowing their limits'? Identities, inequalities and inner city school leavers' post-16 aspirations, *Journal of Education Policy*, 18, 1, 53-69

Askham, P. (2004) *The Feeling's Mutual: Excitement, dread and trust in adult learning and teaching*, Sheffield, Sheffield Hallam University

Atherton, G. and Webster, M. (2003) *Student Retention and Widening Participation in the UK: a case study*, Liverpool Hope University College, Working Paper 25

Austin, M. and Hatt, S. (2005) The Messengers are the Message: A Study of the Effects of Employing Higher Education Student Ambassadors to Work with School Students, *Widening Participation and Lifelong Learning*, 7, 1

Avramidis, E. and Skidmore, D. (2004) Reappraising Learning Support in Higher Education, *Research in Post Compulsory Education*, 9, 1

Bailey, M. (2003) *Ethnic minority participation in British Higher Education: the story of the 1990s*, Northern Ireland: School of Economics and Politics, University of Ulster, Working Paper 10

Ball, S., Reay, D and David, M. (2002) 'Ethnic choosing': minority ethnic students, social class and higher education choice, *Race Ethnicity and Education*, 5, 4, 333-357

Bamber, J. and Tett, L. (1998) Opening the doors of higher education to working-class adults: a case study, *International Journal of Lifelong Education*, 18, 6, 465-7

Bamber, J. and Tett, L. (2000) 'Transforming the learning experiences of non-traditional students: A perspective from higher education, *Studies in Continuing Education*, 22, 1, 57-75

Bamber, J. and Tett, L. (2001) Ensuring integrative learning experiences for non-traditional students, *Widening Participation and Lifelong Learning*, 3, 1, 8-16

Bamber, J., Tett, L., Hosie, E. and Ducklin, A. (1997) Resistance and Determination: working-class adults in higher education, *Research in Post Compulsory Education*, 2, 1

Banks, M., Bates, I., Bynner, J., Breakwell, G., Roberts, K., Emler, N., Jamieson, L. and Roberts, K. (1992) *Careers and identities*, Milton Keynes: Open University Press

Barrett, R. (1999) Why enter compulsory education? White male choice and opportunity in an urban context, *Research in Post-Compulsory Education*, 4,3, 281-303

Battu, H., Belfield, C. and Sloane, P. (2000) How well can we Measure Graduate Over-Education and its Effects?, *National Institute of Economic Review*, 171, 82-93

Beacham, N. and Alty, J. (2004) *An investigation into the effects that digital media can have on the learning outcomes of individuals who have dyslexia*, Mathematics Education Centre, Loughborough University, Working Paper 18

Beaney, P. (2006) *Researching Foundation Degrees: linking research and practice*, London: Foundation Degree Forward Publications

Beck, D., Burgess, G., Gilbert, K., Hodson, R., Hudson, A., Woods, C, and Ivanic, R. (2004) *Listening to learners: practitioner research on the Adult Learners' Lives project*, London: NRDC

Beck, V., Fuller, A. and Unwin, L. (2006) Safety in stereotypes? The impact of gender and 'race' on young people's perceptions of the post-compulsory education and labour market opportunities, *British Educational Research Journal*, 32, 5, 667-686

Becker, G. (1975) *Human Capital: a theoretical and empirical analysis*, Chicago: University of Chicago Press

Beinhart, S. and Smith, P. (1998) *National Adult Learning Survey 1997*, Sudbury: DfEE Publications

Belfield, C. and Morris, Z. (1999) Regional Migration to and from Higher Education Institutions: Scale, Determinants and Outcomes, *Higher Education Quarterly*, 53, 3, 240-63

REFERENCES

Bennett, R. (2003) Determinants of Undergraduate Student Drop Out Rates in a University Business Studies Department, *Journal of Further and Higher Education*, 27, 2

Berggren, C. (2007) Broadening recruitment to higher education through the admission system: gender and class perspectives, *Studies in Higher Education*, 32, 1, 97-116

Biggart, A., Deacon, K., Dobbie, F., Furlong, A., Given, L., and Hinds, K. (2004) *Findings from the Scottish School Leavers Survey: 17 in 2003*, http://www.scotland.gov.uk/library5/education/edrf4-00.asp

Blanden, J., Gregg, P. and Machin, S. (2005) *Intergenerational mobility in Europe and North America: Report for the Sutton Trust*, London: Centre for Economic Performance

Blanden, J., Gregg, P. and MacMillan, L. (2006) *Explaining intergenerational income persistence: non-cognitive skills, ability and education*, CMPO Working Paper Series 06/146

Blasko, Z. (2002) *Access to what: analysis of factors determining graduate employability*, Centre for Higher Education Research

Blundell, R., Dearden, L. and Sianesi, B. (2005) Evaluating the Impact of Education on Earnings in the UK: Models, methods and results from the NCDS, *Journal of the Royal Statistical Society: Series A*

Bond, R. and Saunders, P. (1999) Routes of success: influences on the occupational attainment of young British males, *British Journal of Sociology*, 50, 2, 217-249

Borland, J. and James, S. (1999) The learning experience of students with disabilities in higher education: A case study of a UK university, *Disability and Society*, 14, 1, 85-101

Bowl, M. (2001) Experiencing the barriers: Non-traditional students entering higher education, *Research Papers in Education*, 16, 2, 141-160

Boxall, M., Amin, S., and Baloch, A. (2002) *Determining the Costs of Widening Participation: Report of Pilot Study*, Universities UK/HEFCE

Brooks, R. (2003) Young People's Higher Education Choices: the role of family and friends, British *Journal of Sociology of Education*, 24,3, 283-297

Brooks, R. (2004) 'My mum would be pleased as punch if I went, but my dad is more particular about it': paternal involvement in young people's higher education choices, *British Educational Research Journal*, 30,4, 496-514

Brown, P. and Hesketh, A. (2003) *The social construction of graduate employability*, ESRC research report

Brown, P. and Lauder, H. (1996) Education, globalization and economic development, *Journal of Education Policy*, 11, 1-25

Burchardt, R., Le Grand, J. and Piachaud, D. (1999) Social Exclusion in Britain 1991-1995, *Social Policy and Administration*, 33, 3,227-244

Bynner, J. (1992) ESRC 16-19 Initiative: The route to careers and identities, *ESRC 16-19 Initiative occasional papers* 43, London: City University

Bynner, J. (1998) Youth in the information society: problems, prospects and research directions, *Journal of Education Policy*, 13, 3, 433-442.

Bynner, J., Butler, N., Ferri, E., Shepherd, P. and Smith, K. (2000) *The design and conduct of the 1999-2000 surveys of the National Child Devlopment Study and the 1970 British Cohort Study*, Working Paper 1, London: Centre for Longitudinal Studies

Calder J. (1993) *Disaffection and Diversity: Overcoming barriers to adult learning*, London: Falmer

Callender, C. (2003) *Attitudes to Debt: School leavers and further education students' attitudes to debt and their impact on participation in higher education*, London: Universities UK

Callender, C. and Kemp, M. (2001) *Students in Wales: An analysis of data from the student income and expenditure survey 1998/99*, Cardiff: National Assembly for Wales

Cantwell, R. and Scevak, J. (2004) Engaging university learning: the experiences of students entering university via recognition of prior industrial experience, *Higher Education Research and Development*, 23, 2

Carney-Crompton, S. and Tan, J. (2002) Support systems, psychological functioning, and academic performance of non-traditional female students, *Adult Education Quarterly*, 52, 2, 140-154

Caspi, A., Wright, B., Moffitt, T. and Silva, P.(1998) Early failure in the labour market: childhood and adolescent predictors of unemployment in the transition to adulthood, *American Sociological Review*, 63, 3, 424-51

Castles, J. (2004) Persistence and the Adult Learner: Factors Affecting Persistence in Open University Students, *Active Learning in HE*, 5, 2, 166-179

Cervero, R. and Kirkpatrick, T. (1990) The enduring effects of pre-adult factors on participation in adult education, *American Journal of Education*, 99, 77-94

Chance, J. (2004) *First Year email support and retention*, Aston University

Chapman, B. and Ryan, C. (2002) Income Contingent Financing of Student Higher Education Charges: Assessing the Australian innovation, *Welsh Journal of Education*, 11, 64-81

Chevalier, A. and Conlon, G. (2003) *Does it pay to attend a prestigious university?*, CEE Discussion Papers 0033, Centre for the Economics of Education, LSE

Chevalier, A. and Walker, I. (2001) The United Kingdom, in Harmon, C., Walker, I and Westergaard-Neilson, N. (eds.) *Education and Earnings in Europe: A Cross-Country Analysis of the Returns to Education*, Edward Elgar: Cheltenham

Christie, H., Munro, M. and Wagner, F. (2005) 'Day students' in higher education: widening access students and successful transitions to university life, *International Studies in Sociology of Education*, 15, 1, 3-29

Clancy, J. (2005) Billions 'wasted' on Skills for Life, *Times Educational Supplement FE Focus*, 9/12/05, p.1

Clegg, S., Hudson, A., and Steel, J. (2003) The Emperor's New Clothes: globalisation and e-learning in Higher Education, *British Journal of Sociology of Educaiton*, 24, 1, 39-53

Coffield, F. (1997) *'A national strategy for lifelong learning'* Newcastle upon Tyne: Department of Education, University of Newcastle

Coffield, F. (1999) Breaking the Consensus: lifelong learning as social control, *British Educational Research Journal*, 25, 479-500

Collier, T., Gilchrist, R., Phillips, D. (2003) Who plans to Go to University? Statistical Modelling of Potential Working-Class Participants, *Educational Research and Evaluation*, 9, 3, 239-263

Conlon, G. (2001) *The incidence and outcomes associated with the late attainment of qualifications in the United Kingdom*, CEE Discussion Papers 0013, Centre for the Economics of Education, LSE

Connelly, G. and Chakrabarti, M. (1999) Access courses and students from minority ethnic backgrounds, *Journal of Further and Higher Education*, 23, 2, 231-44

Connor, H. (2001) Deciding for or against participation in Higher Education: the views of young people from lower social backgrounds, *Higher Education Quarterly*, 55,2, 202-224

Connor, H. and Dewson, S. (2001) Social class and higher education: issues affecting decisions on participation by lower social class groups, *DfEE Research Report* 267

Connor, H., Burton, R., Pearson, R., Pollard, E. and Regan, J. (1999) *Making the right choice: How students choose universities and colleges*, London: Universities UK

Connor, H., Tyers, C. and Modood, T. (2004) *Why the difference? A closer look at Higher Education minority ethnic students and graduates*, London: DfES, 216

Cooke, R., Barkham, M., Audin, K., Bradley, M. and Davy, J. (2004) How social class differences affect students' experience of university, *Journal of Further and Higher Education*, 28, 4, 407-421

Croll, P. and Moses, D. (2003) *Young people's trajectories into post-compulsory education and training: a preliminary analysis of data from the British Household Panel Survey*, paper presented at the Annual Conference of the British Educational Research Association, Heriot-Watt University, Edinburgh, 10-13th September 2003

Croucher, K., Evans, M. and Leacy, A. (2005) *What happens next? A report on the first destinations of 2003 graduates with disabilities*, Association of Graduate Careers Advisory Services Disability Development Network

Croxford, L. (2006) *The Youth Cohort Surveys – how good is the evidence?*, Edinburgh: Education Youth and Transitions Project

Dearden, L., Emmerson, C., Frayne, C. and Meghir, C. (2005) *Education Subsidies and School Drop-out Rates*, IFS Working Paper W05/11

Dearden, L., McGranahan, L. and Sianesi, B. (2004a) *The Role of Credit Constraints in Educational Choices: evidence from NCDS and BCS70*, London School of Economics and Political Science, Centre for the Economics of Education Discussion Paper No. 48

Dearden, L., McGranahan, L. and Sianesi, B. (2004b) *Returns to Education for the 'Marginal Learner': evidence from the BCS70*, London School of Economics, Centre for the Economics of Education, Discussion Paper No. 45

Dearden, L., McIntosh, S., Myck, M. and Vignoles, A. (2002) The Returns to Academic and Vocational Qualifications in Britain, *Bulletin of Economic Research*, 54, 249-74

Dearing R. (1997) *Higher Education in the learning society. Report of the Committee under the Chairmanship of Sir Ron Dearing*, London, Stationery Office

Denholm, J. and Macleod, D. (2003) *Prospects for growth in further education*, Wellington: Learning and Skills Research Centre

Department for Education and Employment (1995) *Training Statistics 1995*, London: HMSO

Department for Education and Employment (1998) *The Learning Age: a renaissance for a new Britain*, London: Stationery Office

Department for Education and Skills (2003) *Widening participation in higher education*, London: Department for Education and Skills

Department for Trade and Industry (1998) *Our Competitive Future: building the knowledge driven economy*, White Paper December 1998, London, Stationery Office

Dhillon, J. (2004) An exploration of adult learners' perspectives of using learndirect centres as sites of learning, *Research in Post-Compulsory Education*, 9, 1, 147-158

Dodgson, R. and Bolam, H. (2002) *Student retention, support and widening participation in the North East of England*, Universities for the North East, (www.unis4ne.ac.uk/unew/Projects AdditionalFiles/wp/Retention_report.pdf, checked on 15/06/05)

Dodgson, R. and Whitham, H. (2004) *Learner experience of foundation degrees in the North East of England: Access, support and retention*, Draft report (September)

Dolton P. and Silles, M. (2001) *Over-Education in the Graduate Labour Market*, Centre for Economics of Education

Donaldson, J. and Graham, S. (1999) A Model of College Outcomes for Adults, *Adult Education Quarterly*, 50, 1, 24-40

Dunlop, C. and Burtch, B. (2003) Doors close, windows open: a British Columbia case study on widening access, *Journal of Adult and Continuing Education*, 9, 1

Dynarski, S. (2003) Does Aid matter? Measuring the effect of student aid on college attendance and performance, *American Economic Review*, 92, 2, 279-88

Ecclestone, K. (2006) Let the poor do hairdressing, *Times Educational Supplement FE Focus*, 9/6/06, p.6

Edmonds, S., Archer, T., Macaulay, A. and Kendall, L. (2003) *Evaluation of the 2002 DfES/Sutton Trust FE2HE Summer Schools – Final Report*, National Foundation for Educational Research, 115

Education and Employment Committee (2001) *Higher Education Access*, Fourth Report, HC 124, London: House of Commons

Edwards, R., Sieminski, S. and Zeldin, D. (1993) *Adult Learners, Education and Training*, London: Routledge

Egerton, M. and Parry, G. (2001) Lifelong Debt: Rates of Return to Mature Study, *Higher Education Quarterly*, 55, 1, 4

Emmerson, C, Frayne, C., McNally, S. and Silva, O. (2005) *Economic Evaluation of Opportunity Bursaries, Evaluation of Aimhigher: Excellence Challenge*, Department for Education and Skills

ETAG (1999) *An education and training action plan for Wales*, Cardiff: ETAG

European Commission (2001) *Making a European area of lifelong learning a reality*, DG Education and Culture, European Commission Communication

European Group for Research on Equity in Educational Systems, (2005) Equity in European Educational Systems: a set of indicators, *European Educational Research Journal*, 4, 2, 1-151

Feinstein, L. (2003) Nursery or bursary, *Times Higher Educational Supplement*, 12/12/03, p.16

Feinstein, L., Duckworth, K. and Sabates, R. (2004) *A model of inter-generational effects of parental education*, Research Brief RCB01-04, Nottingham: DfES

FEU (1993) *Paying their way: the experiences of adult learners in vocational education and training in FE Colleges*, London: Further Education Unit

Fevre, R., Rees, G. and Gorard, S. (1999) Some sociological alternatives to Human Capital Theory, *Journal of Education and Work*, 12, 2, 117-140

Forsyth, A. and Furlong, A. (2003) *Socio-economic disadvantage and access to higher education* Bristol: Policy Press

Foskett, N. (2002) Marketing Imperative or Cultural Challenge? Embedding Widening Participation in the Further Education Sector, *Research in Post Compulsory Education*, 7, 1

Francis, B. (1999) 'You can never get too much education': the discourses used by secondary school students in their discussion of post-compulsory education, *Research in Post-Compulsory Education*, 4,3, 305-319

Fryer, R. (1997) *Learning for the Twenty-First Century*, London: Department of Education and Employment

Fuller, M., Healey, M., Bradley, A. and Hall, T. (2004) Barriers to learning: a systematic study of the experience of disabled students in one university, *Studies in Higher Education*, 29, 3

Furlong, A. (2005) Cultural dimensions of decisions about educational participation among 14- to 19-year-olds, *Journal of Education Policy*, 20, 3, 379-389

Gambetta D. (1987) *Were they pushed or did they jump? Individual decision mechanisms in education*, London: Cambridge University Press

Garner L. and Imeson R. (1996) More Bricks in the Wall: The ending of the Older Students' Allowance and the new '16 Hour Rule'. Has the cost of higher education for mature students finally got too high?, *Journal of Access Studies*, 11, 97-110

George, J., Cowan, J., Hewitt, L. and Cannell, P. (2004) Failure dances to the tune of insecurity: affective issues in the assessment and evaluation of access learning, *Journal of Access Policy and Practice*, 1, 2

Gerber, T. and Hout, M. (1995) Educational stratification in Russia during the Soviet period, *American Journal of Sociology,* 101, 611-660

Gerrard, E. and Roberts, R. (2006) Student parents, hardship and debt: a qualitative study, *Journal of Further and Higher Education,* 30, 4, 393-403

Glass, D. (1954) *Social mobility in Britain,* London: Routledge

Glover, D., Law, S. and Youngman, A. (2002) Graduateness and Employability: student perceptions of the personal outcomes of university education, *Research in Post Compulsory Education,* 7, 3

Goddard, A. (2004) Subjects slot into class divide, *Times Higher Educational Supplement,* 30/4/04, p.1 and 8-9

Goddard, A. and Utley, A. (2004) Review 'papers over cracks', *Times Higher Educational Supplement,* 9/4/04, p.1

Gorard, S. (1997) *Initial Educational Trajectories. Patterns of participation in adult education and training. Working paper 8,* Cardiff: School of Education

Gorard, S. (2000) *Education and Social Justice,* Cardiff: University of Wales Press

Gorard, S. (2001) International comparisons of school effectiveness: a second component of the 'crisis account'?, *Comparative Education,* 37, 3, 279-296

Gorard, S. (2002a) Fostering scepticism: the importance of warranting claims, *Evaluation and Research in Education,* 16, 3, 136-149

Gorard, S. (2002b) The role of causal models in education as a social science, *Evaluation and Research in Education,* 16, 1, 51-65

Gorard, S. (2002c) Political control: A way forward for educational research?, *British Journal of Educational Studies,* 50, 3, 378-389

Gorard, S. (2002d) Ethics and equity: pursuing the perspective of non-participants, *Social Research Update,* 39, 1-4

Gorard, S. (2003) *Quantitative methods in social science: the role of numbers made easy,* London: Continuum

Gorard, S. (2005a) Where shall we widen it? Higher Education and the age participation rate in Wales, *Higher Education Quarterly,* 59, 1, 3-18

Gorard, S. (2005b) Academies as the 'future of schooling': is this an evidence-based policy?, *Journal of Education Policy,* 20, 3, 369-377

Gorard, S. (2006a) Towards a judgement-based statistical analysis, *British Journal of Sociology of Education,* 27, 1, 67-80

Gorard, S. (2006b) Does policy matter in education?, *International Journal of Research and Method in Education,* 29, 1, 5-21

Gorard, S. and Rees, G. (2002) *Creating a learning society?,* Bristol: Policy Press

Gorard, S. and Smith, E. (2004) What is 'underachievement' at school?, *School Leadership and Management,* 24, 2, 205-225

Gorard, S. and Smith, E. (2006) Beyond the 'learning society': what have we learnt from widening participation research?, *International Journal of Lifelong Education,* 25, 6, 575-594

Gorard, S. and Taylor, C. (2001) *Student funding and hardship in Wales: a statistical summary, Report to the National Assembly Investigation Group on Student Hardship,* Cardiff: National Assembly for Wales

Gorard, S., Rees, G. and Fevre, R. (1999a) Two dimensions of time: the changing social context of lifelong learning, *Studies in the Education of Adults,* 31, 1, 35-48

Gorard, S., Rees, G. and Fevre, R. (1999b) Patterns of participation in lifelong learning: do families make a difference?, *British Educational Research Journal,* 25, 4, 517-532

Gorard, S., Fevre, R. and Rees, G. (1999c) The apparent decline of informal learning, *Oxford Review of Education*, 25, 4, 437-454

Gorard, S., Rees, G. and Salisbury, J. (2001a) The differential attainment of boys and girls at school: investigating the patterns and their determinants, *British Educational Research Journal*, 27, 2, 125-139

Gorard, S., Rees, G., Fevre, R. and Welland, T. (2001b) Lifelong learning trajectories: some voices of those in transit, *International Journal of Lifelong Education*, 20, 3, 169-187

Gorard, S., Rees, G. and Selwyn, N. (2002a) The 'conveyor belt effect': a re-assessment of the impact of National Targets for Lifelong Learning, *Oxford Review of Education*, 28, 1, 75-89

Gorard, S., Selwyn, N. and Rees, G. (2002b) Privileging the visible: Examining the National Targets for Education and Training, *British Educational Research Journal*, 28, 3, 309-325

Gorard, S., Selwyn, N. and Madden, L. (2003) Logged on to learning? Assessing the impact of technology on participation in lifelong learning, *International Journal of Lifelong Education*, 22, 3, 281-296

Gorard, S., Rushforth, K. and Taylor, C. (2004a) Is there a shortage of quantitative work in education research?, *Oxford Review of Education*, 30, 3, 371-395

Gorard, S., Lewis, J. and Smith, E. (2004b) Disengagement in Wales: Educational, social and economic issues, *Welsh Journal of Education,* 13, 1, 118-147

Gorard, S., Smith, E. Thomas, E., May, H., Adnett, N. and Slack, K. (2006) *Review of widening participation research: addressing the barriers to participation in higher education*, London: HEFCE, 170 pages, available at http://195.194.167.100/pubs/rdreports/2006/rd13_06/

Greater Merseyside Aimhigher (2003) *Stimulating and Sustaining Interest and Achievement in Maths and Science* – an evaluative report of the activities of the Edge Hill strand of Aimhigher Greater Merseyside, 2000-2002, Greater Merseyside: Aimhigher Greater Merseyside

Greenaway, D. and Haynes, M. (2004) Funding Higher Education, in G. Johnes and J. Johnes (eds.) *International Handbook on the Economics of Education,* Cheltenham: Edward Elgar Publishing

Gutteridge, R. (2001) *Student support, guidance and retention: re-defining additional needs*, Coventry University, 16

Hall, J. and Tinklin, T. (1998) *Students First: the experience of disabled students in HE,* The SCRE Centre

Hall, T. and Healey, M. (2004) *The Experience of Learning at University by Disabled Students in Geography, Earth and Environmental Sciences and Related Disciplines* – Report on the Inclusive Curriculum Project (ICP) Student Survey, Geography Discipline Network

Halsey, A., Heath, A. and Ridge, J. (1980) *Origins and Destinations: Family, Class, and Education in Modern Britain,* Oxford: Clarendon

Hammer, T. (2003) The Probability for Unemployed Young People to Re-Enter Education or Employment: a comparative study in six Northern European countries, *British Journal of Sociology of Education*, 24, 2, 209-23

Hand, A., Gambles, J. and Cooper, E. (1994) *Individual Commitment to Learning. Individuals decision-making about lifelong learning,* Employment Department

Harris, R. and Fallows, S. (2002) Enlarging Educational Opportunity: summer-semester provision in UK higher education, *Quality in Higher Education*, 8, 3, 225-37.

Harrison R. (1993) Disaffection and access, in Calder J. (Ed.) *Disaffection and diversity. Overcoming barriers to adult learning,* London: Falmer

Harrison, N. (2006) The impact of negative experiences, dissatisfaction and attachment on first year underdraduate withdrawal, *Journal of Further and Higher Education*, 30, 4, 377-391

Harvey, M. and Slaughter, T. (2007) Evaluation of an access route to higher education through a work-based assessment strategy, *Assessment and Evaluation in Higher Education*, 32, 1, 35-43

Hatt, S. and Baxter, A. (2003) From FE to HE: Studies in transition, *Journal of Widening Participation and Lifelong Learning*, 5, 2, 18-29

Hatt, S., Hannan, A. and Baxter, A. (2005a) Bursaries and Student Success: a study of students from low-income groups at two institutions in the South West, *Higher Education Quarterly*, 59, 2, 111-26

Hatt, S., Hannan, A., Baxter, A. and Harrison, N. (2005b) Opportunity Knocks? The impact of bursary schemes on students from low-income backgrounds, *Studies in Higher Education*, 30, 4, 373-88

Hayes, K. and King, E. (1997) Mature students in higher education: III. Approaches to studying in Access students, *Studies in Higher Education*, 22, 1

Helmsley-Brown, J. (1999) College Choice: perceptions and priorities, *Educational Management and Administration*, 27, 1, 85-98

Higher Education Funding Council for England (2001) *Strategies for Widening Participation in Higher Education: A guide to good practice*, HEFCE 01/36

Higher Education Funding Council for England (2005) *Young participation in higher education*, Bristol: Higher Education Funding Council for England

Higher Education Funding Council for England (2006) http://www.hefce.ac.uk/aboutus/glossary/glossary.htm, accessed 4th April 2006

Higher Education Funding Council for Wales (2000) *Participation rates for Welsh students in Higher Education within the UK during 1997/98,* Cardiff: Higher Education Funding Council for Wales

Higson, H., Nai, L. and Sushmita, J. (2003) *Research and design of programmes that attract and fulfil the needs of Britain's ethnic groups,* Report for Aston University's Business School

Hills, J. (2003) *Stakeholder perceptions of the employability of non-traditional students,* London: London Metropolitan University, 44

Hoad, J. (2001) NPC/98/10/B: *Widening participation in higher education: funding proposals HEFCE consultation 98/39,* Summary of responses sought and submission from the National Postgraduate Committee (NPC), Accessed on line 28/7/05

Hogarth, T., Purcell, K., and Wilson, R. (1997) *The Participation of Non-traditional Students in Higher Education,* London: IER for HEFCE, 207

Holdsworth, C. and Patiniotis, J. (2004) *The choices and experiences of higher education students living in the parental home,* http://www.liv.ac.uk/geography/research/grants/stay_at_home.htm

Hoskins, S. and Newstead, S. (1997) Degree performance as a function of age, gender, prior qualifications and discipline studied, *Assessment and Evaluation in Higher Education*, 22, 3

Howieson, C. and Iannelli, C. (2003) *The effects of low attainment on young people's outcomes at age 22-23 in Scotland,* Paper presented at the British Educational Research Association Annual Conference, Heriot-Watt University, Edinburgh, 11-13th September 2003

Hramiak, A. (2001) *Widening participation and ethnic minority women,* Annual SCUTREA Conference proceedings

Hudson, C. (2005a) *Widening participation in higher education art and design: Part 1 literature review,* Winchester: Council for Higher Education in Art and Design

Hudson, C. (2005b) *Widening participation in higher education art and design: Part 2 Questionnaire report,* Winchester: Council for Higher Education in Art and Design

Hutton, J. (2005) *Young participation in higher education: England to learn from Wales, Northern Ireland and Scotland,* University of Warwick Department of Statistics, mimeo

James, D. (2001) Making the graduate: perspectives on student experience of assessment in higher education, in A. Filer (ed.), *Assessment: Social Practice, social product*, London: Routledge

James, J. and Preece, J. (2002) *Was IT good for you? Women returners and the immediate and delayed impact of ICT training on their return to work or education*, Paper presented at the European Conference on Educational Research, University of Lisbon, 11-14 September 2002

James, R. (2002) *Socioeconomic Background and Higher Education Participation: An analysis of school students' aspirations and expectations*, Canberra: DEST Higher Education Group Evaluations and Investigations Programme

Jantti, M., Bratsberg, B., Roed, K., Raaum, O., Naylor, R., Osterbacka, E., Bjorklund, A. and Erikson, T. (2006) *American exceptionalism in a new light: a comparison of intergenerational earnings mobility in the Nordic countries, the United Kingdom and the United States*, IZA Discussion Paper 1938

Johnes, G. and McNabb, R. (2004) Never Give Up on the Good Times: Student Attrition in the UK, *Oxford Bulletin of Economic Research*, 66, 23-47

Jones, P. and Abramson, M. (2003) Keeping under-represented students: a case study in early engagement, in D. Saunders, R. Payne, H. Jones, A. Mason and J. Storan (eds.) *Attracting and Retaining Learners: Policy and Practice Perspectives*, FACE: 188-201

Kahn, P. and Macdonald, R. (2004) *Reviews of the impact of staff and educational development: a means to improve the scholarly basis for our practice*, presentation to Staff and Educational Developers Annual Conference, November, see http://www.seda.ac.uk/confs/birmingham04/birmingham2004-2.htm

Kay, H. and Sundaraj, A. (2004) Are Undergraduate Mature Students Widening Participation Students?, in D. Saunders, K. Brosnan, M. Walker *et al* (eds.) *Learning Transformations: Changing Learners, Organisations and Communities*, London: Forum for the Advancement of Continuing Education: 255-260

Keep, E. and Mayhew, K. (2004) The Economic and Distributional Implications of Current Policies on Higher Education, *Oxford Review of Economic Policy*, 20, 2, 298-314

Kelly, R. (2006) *Social mobility: narrowing social class educational attainment gaps*, presentation to IPPR, 26/4/06

Kelly, T. (1992) *A History of Adult Education in Great Britain,* Liverpool: Liverpool University Press

Kember, D., Lee, K. and Li. N. (2001) Cultivating a sense of belonging in part-time students, *International Journal of Lifelong Education,* 20, 4, 326-341

Kennedy, H. (1997) *Learning Works: widening participation in further education*, Coventry: Further Education Funding Council

Kerkvliet, J. and Nowell, C. (2005) Does One Size Fit All? University differences in the influence of wages, financial aid, and integration on student retention, *Economics of Education Review*, 24, 1, 85-95

Kingston, P. (2004) Adults learning less under Labour, *The Guardian, Education Supplement*, p.15

Knowles, J. (1997) *The influence of socio-economic status on aspirations to enter HE*, paper presented at the Annual Conference of the British Educational Research Association, University of York, 11-14 September 1997

Knox, H. and McGillivray, A. (2005) Students helping students, in Acland, A. *et al* (eds.) *Access, Retention and Employability: Transforming Higher Education* (FACE).

Lambert, P. (2002) Handling occupational information, *Building Research Capacity*, 4, pp.9-12

Lawy, R. (2000) Is Jimmy Really so Different? Learning and making-meaning in work and non-work contexts, *British Journal of Sociology of Education*, 21, 4, 591-604

Layer, G., Srivastava, A., Thomas, L. and Yorke, M. (2002) Student success: Building for change (www.actiononaccess.org/resource/aoadocs/ssintro.doc, checked on 15/06/05)

Learning from Experience Trust (LET) (2003) *Extending participation to socially excluded and marginalised sections of society, The Learning from Experience Trust*, Goldsmiths College, 7

Leathwood, C. (2004) A Critique of Institutional Inequalities in Higher Education (or an Alternative to Hypocrisy for Higher Educational Policy), *Theory and Research in Education*, 2, 1, 31-48

Leathwood, C. and O'Connell, P. (2003) It's a struggle': the construction of the 'new student' in higher education, *Journal of Education Policy*, 18, 6, 597-615

Lee, C. (2003) Why we need to re-think race and ethnicity in educational research, *Educational Researcher*, 32, 5, 3-5

Lee, J. (2006a) Free courses failed to reel in adult learners, *Times Educational Supplement FE Focus*, 23/6/06, p.1

Lee, J. (2006b) Minister gives way on adult learning, *Times Educational Supplement FE Focus*, 28/1/06, p.1

Leslie, D. and Lindley, J. (2001) The Impact of Language Ability on Employment and Earnings of Britain's Ethnic Communities, *Economica*, 68, 272, 587

Leslie, D., Abbot, A. and Blackaby, D. (2002) Why are ethnic minority applicants less likely to be accepted into higher education?, *Higher Education Quarterly*, 56, 1, 65-91

Liverpool Hope University College (2003) *Stepping Stones Residential at Liverpool Hope University College* – Monday 28th July – Wednesday 30th July 2003 – Evaluation, Liverpool Hope University College, 24.

Livingstone, D. (2000) Researching expanded notions of learning and work and underemployment: findings of the first Canadian survey of informal learning practices, *International Review of Education*, 46, 6, 491-514

Long, M. and Hayden, M. (2001) *Paying Their Way: A survey of undergraduate student finances, 2000*, Canberra: Australian Vice-Chancellor's Committee

Longden, B. (2000) Élitism to Inclusion – Some Developmental Tension, *Educational Studies*, 26, 4, 455-74

Loots, C., Osborne, M., and Seagraves, L. (1998) Learning at Work – Work-based Access to Higher Education, *The Journal of Continuing Higher Education*, 46, 1, 16-30

Lowe, J. (1970) *Adult Education in England and Wales: A critical survey*, London: Michael Joseph

Lumby, J., Foskett, N. and Maringe, F. (2003) *Choice, pathways and progression for young people in West London*, A report to London West Learning and Skills Council, University of Lincoln

Macleod, D. (2003) *Widening adult participation: a review of research and development*, London: Learning and Skills Development Agency

Macleod, F. and Lambe, P. (2006) *Who amongst initial phase leavers in England is least likely to return to adult learning?*, BERA, Warwick, September 2006

Maguire, M., Ball, S. and Macrae, S. (1999) Promotion, Persuasion and Class-taste: marketing (in) the UK post-compulsory sector, *British Journal of Sociology of Education*, 20, 3, 291-308

Maguire, M., Maguire, S. and Felstead, A. (1993) *Factors Influencing Individual Commitment to Lifelong Learning*, Research Series No.20, Sheffield: Employment Department

Mangan, J., Adnett, N. and Davies, P. (2001) Movers and Stayers: determinants of post-16 educational choice, *Research in Post-Compulsory Education*, 6, 1, 31-50

Manski, C. (1989) Schooling as Experimentation: A reappraisal of the post secondary dropout phenomenon, *Economics of Education Review*, 8, 4, 305-312

Marks, A. (2000) Lifelong Learning and the 'Breadwinner Ideology': addressing the problems of lack of participation by adult, working-class males in higher education on Merseyside, *Educational Studies*, 26, 3, 303-19

Marsh, C. and Blackburn R (1992) Class Differences in Access to Higher Education in Britain, in Burrows, R. and Marsh, C. (eds.) *Consumption and Class: divisions and change*, London: Macmillan

Marsick, V. and Watkins, K. (1990) *Informal and incidental learning in the workplace*, London: Routledge

Martinez, P. (2001) *Improving student retention and achievement: what do we know and what do we need to find out?*, Learning and Skills Development Agency

May, S. and Bousted, M. (2004) *Investigation of student retention through an analysis of first year students at Kingston University*, Staffordshire University

Mayhew, K., Deer, C. and Dua, M. (2004) The move to mass higher education in the UK, *Oxford Review of Education*, 30, 1, 65-82

Mayo, M. (2002) *Action Learning in the Community*, http://www.goldsmiths.ac.uk/cucr/html/research.html

McAuley, A (2004) Learning About Learners: Understanding the Student Experience', in D. Saunders, K. Brosnan, M. Walker *et al* (eds.) *Learning Transformations: Changing Learners, Organisations and Communities*, London: Forum for the Advancement of Continuing Education:378-86

McGillivray, A. and Knox, H. (2003) *Student Diversity – Participation and Progress*, University of Paisley

McGivney, V. (1990) *Education's for Other People: Access to Education for Non-Participant Adults*, Leicester: NIACE

McGivney, V. (1992) *Motivating unemployed adults to undertake education and training*, Leicester: National Institute of Adult Continuing Education

McGivney, V. (1993) Participation and non-participation. A review of the literature, in Edwards, R., Sieminski, S. and Zeldin, D. (eds.) *Adult Learners, Education and Training*, London: Routledge

McGrath, S. and Millen, P. (2004) *Getting them in: An investigation of factors affecting progression of HE pf 16-19 year olds in full-time education*, Manchester Metropolitan University and the LSDA

McGuinness, S. (2003) University Quality and Labour Market Outcomes, *Applied Economics*, 35, 1943-55

McIntosh, S. (2004) *Further Analysis of the Returns to Academic and Vocational Qualification, Department for Education and Skills*, Research Report No. 370, HMSO: Norwich

McLinden, M. (2003) Children into university: an outreach project working with school years 8 – 13, in Saunder, D., Payne, R., Jones, H., Mason, A. and Storan, J. (eds.) *Attracting and Retaining Learners: Policy and Practice Perspectives*. FACE

Mercer, J. and Saunders, D. (2004) Accomodating Change: the process of growth and development amongst a mature student population, *Research in Post-Compulsory Education*, 9, 2, 283-299

Merrell, C. and Tymms, P. (2005) *The impact of early interventions and pre-school experience on the cognitive development of young children in England*, presentation at American Educational Research Association Annual Conference, Montreal, April 2005

Merrill, B. (2001) Learning and Teaching in Universities: perspectives from adult learners and lecturers, *Teaching in Higher Education*, 6, 1, 5-17

Metcalf, H. (2005) Paying for University: The impact of increasing costs on student employment, debt and satisfaction, *National Institute Economic Review*, 191(January), 106-117

REFERENCES

Moogan, Y., Baron, S. and Harris, K. (1999) Decision-making behaviour of potential Higher Education students, *Higher Education Quarterly*, 53, 3, 211-228

Moor, H., Bedford, N., Johnson, A., Hall, M., Harland, J. (2004) *Moving Forward: Thinking Back: Young People's Post-16 Paths and Perspectives on Education, Training and Employment*, The Post-16 Phase of the Northern Ireland Curriculum Cohort Study: Full Report, NFER

Morgan, S. and P. Lister (2004) The Changing Face of Induction. Learning, in D. Saunders, K. Brosnan, M. Walker *et al* (eds.) *Transformations: Changing Learners, Organisations and Communities,* London, Forum for the Advancement of Continuing Education: 21-26

Morris, M., Golden, S., Ireland, E. and Judkins, M. (2005a) *Evaluation of Aimhigher: Excellence Challenge. The Views of Partnership Coordinators 2004* (DfES Research Report 650), London: DfES

Morris, M., Rutt, S. and Yeshanew, T. (2005b) *Evaluation of Aimhigher: Excellence Challenge. Pupil Outcomes One Year On* (DfES Research Report 649), London: DfES

Murphy, H. and Roopchand, N. (2003) Intrinsic Motivation and Self-esteem in Traditional and Mature Students at a Post-1992 University in the North-east of England, *Educational Studies*, 29, 2, 243-259

Murphy, M. (2000) *How the other half lives: A case study of successful and unsuccessful mature applicants in Irish higher education.* Paper presented at SCUTREA, 30th Annual Conference, 3-5 July, 2000, University of Nottingham

Murphy, M. and Fleming, T. (2000) Between common and college knowledge: exploring the boundaries between adult and higher education, *Studies in Continuing Education*, 22, 1, 77-93

Musselbrook, K. (2003) *Students' experience of university: some interim findings,* South East of Scotland Wider Access Regional Forum (SESWARF): 2

NACETT (1994) *Review of the National Targets for Education and Training: Proposals for Consultation,* London: NACETT

Nash, R. (2005) Cognitive habitus and collective intelligence, *Journal of Education Policy*, 20, 1, 3-21

National Audit Office (2002) *Widening participation in higher education in England,* London: The Stationery Office

National Compact Scheme Project (2005) *Preliminary Report*, http://www.leeds.ac.uk/external-affairs/city/NCS per cent20Report.pdf, accessed 20th September 2005

National Statistics (2001) *Higher Education students: population profiles 1999/2000*, Cardiff: National Assembly for Wales

Naylor, R. and Smith, J. (2004) Determinants of Educational Success in Higher Education, in G. Johnes and J. Johnes (eds.) *International Handbook on the Economics of Education*, Edward Elgar: Cheltenham, 415-61

Nettle, D. (2003) Intelligence and class mobility in the British population, *British Journal of Psychology,* 94, 551-561

NIACE (1994) *Widening Participation: Routes to a learning society*, NIACE Policy Discussion Paper

NIACE (2000) *The learning divide revisited*, Leicester: National Institute for Adult and Continuing Education

NIACE (2003) *Adults Learning Survey – 2003,* Leicester, National Institute for Adult and Continuing Education

Noble, J. (2004) *Student responses to early leaving*, www.staffs.ac.uk/institutes/access/docs/28604 uk2.doc, checked on 15/06/07

Noble, M. Ingraham, B. and Dale, A. (2003) Widening participation through on-line learning: Using LearnDirect (UFI) to support accredited learning, in Saunders, D., Payne, R., Jones, H., Mason, A. and Storan, J. (eds.) *Attracting and Retaining Learners: Policy and Practice Perspectives*. FACE

OECD (2003) *Beyond rhetoric: adult learning policies and practices*, Paris, OECD

Osborne, M. (2003) Policy and practice in widening participation: a six country comparative study of access as flexibility, *International Journal of Lifelong Education*, 22, 1, 43-58

Osborne, R. and Leith, H. (2000), 'Evaluation of the targeted initiative on widening access for young people from socio-economically disadvantaged backgrounds.' (Dublin: Higher Education Authority), 82

Otterson, E. (2004) Lifelong learning and challenges posed to European labour markets, *European Journal of Education*, 39, 2, 151-157

Ozga, J. and Sukhnandan, S. (1998) Undergraduate non-completion: Developing an explanatory model, *Higher Education Quarterly*, 53, 3, 316-333

Panesar, J. (2003) Life Testimony Perspectives from Asian Women Learners, in D. Saunders, *et al* (eds.) *Attracting and Retaining Learners: Policy and Practice Perspectives*, 86-99

Park, A. (1994) *Individual Commitment to Lifelong Learning: Individuals attitudes*. Report on the quantitative survey, Employment Department

Parkinson, M. (1998) *Combating Social Exclusion: Lessons from Area-Based Programmes in Europe*, York, Joseph Rowntree Foundation

Payne, J. (1998) *Routes at Sixteen: Trends and Choices in the Nineties*, London: DfES Research brief No 55

Payne, J. (2001) *Patterns of Participation in Full-time Education after 16: An analysis of the England and Wales Youth Cohort Study*, DfES Report, http://www.dfes.gov.uk/research/data/ uploadfiles/ RR307.PDF

Payne, R., Saunders, D., and Jones, C. (2005), Engaging learners in traditional areas of non-participation in education – The Llynfi Valley project, in A. Acland, *et al* (eds.), *Access, Retention and Employability: Transforming Higher Education*, FACE

Peasgood, A (2004) Gateway or Obstacle? Reflections Upon the Role of Assessment in Widening Participation, in D Saunders, *et al* (eds.), *Learning Transformations: Changing Learners, Organisations and Communities*, London: Forum for the Advancement of Continuing Education, 364-69

Pennell, H, West, A, and Hind, A (2005) Survey of Higher Education Providers 2004, *Evaluation of Aimhigher: Excellence Challenge*, Department for Education and Skills

Pennell, H., West, A. and Hind, A. (2004) *The national evaluation of Aimhigher: Survey of higher education providers*, DfES Research Report RR537

People and Work Unit (2004) *Evaluation of the Progression through Partnership Project – Final Report*, Newport: University of Wales College, 23

Pettigrew, A., Hendry, C. and Sparrow, P. (1989) *Training in Britain. A study of funding, activity and attitudes. Employers perspectives on human resources*. London: HMSO

Pickerden, A. (2002) Muslim women in Higher Education: new sites of lifelong learning, *International Journal of Lifelong Education*, 21, 1, 37-43

Pitcher, J. and Purcell, K. (1998) Diverse Expectations and Access to Opportunities: is there a graduate labour market?, *Higher Education Quarterly*, 52, 2, 179-203

Postle, G., Sturman, A. and Clarke, J. (2002) Australia. In *Widening Participation in Higher Education: Report to Scottish Executive, Part 2, Country Studies*. Stirling: Centre for Research in Lifelong

Povey, H. and Angier, C. (2004) *'I can do it, but it'll be a battle': finding her place as an undergraduate mathematician*, Sheffield Hallam University

Power, S., Rees, G. and Taylor, C. (2005) New Labour and educational disadvantage: the limits of area-based initiatives, *London Review of Education*, 3, 2, 101-116

Powney, J. (2002) *Successful student diversity: Case studies of practice in learning and teaching and widening participation*, HEFCE: 33

Prospects (2002) *Widening participation in higher education*, http://www.prospects.ac.uk/cms/ShowPage/Home_page/Labour_market_information/Graduate_Market_Trends/Widening_participation_in_higher_education__Spring_02_/p!eLdXgb;DCC1$3, accessed 20/5/05

Prospects (2005) *Progress on widening participation in higher education*, http://www.prospects.ac.uk/cms/ShowPage/Home_page/Labour_market_information/Graduate_Market_Trends/Progress_on_widening_participation_in_HE__Spring_05_/p!eeXLbpm;$3F$3F$3, accessed 20/5/05

Purcell, K. and Hogarth, T. (1999) *Graduate Opportunities, Social Class and Age: Employers' Recruitment Strategies in the new graduate labour market*, CIHE

Purcell, K., Morley, M. and Rowley, G. (2002) *Employers in the New Graduate Labour Market: recruiting from a wider spectrum of graduates,* Bristol: Employment Studies Unit, University of the West of England

Pustjens, H., Van de Gaer, E., Van Damme, J. and Onghena, P. (2004) Effect of secondary schools on academic choices and on success in higher education, *School Effectiveness and School Improvement,* 15, 3/4, 281-311

Quicke, J. (1997) Reflexivity, community and education for the learning society, *Curriculum Studies*, 5, 2, 139-161

Raffe, D. (2000) *Young People Not in Education, Employment or Training*, Edinburgh: CES Briefing Paper 29, http://www.ed.ac.uk/ces/PDF per cent20Files/Brief029.pdf

Raffe, D., Croxford, L., Ianelli, I. Shapira, M. and Howieson, C. (2006) *Social class inequalities in Education in England and Scotland*, Edinburgh: Education Youth and Transitions Project

Raffe, D., Fairgrieve, K., and Martin, C. (2001) Participation, Inclusiveness, Academic Drift and Parity of Esteem: a comparison of post-compulsory education and training in England, Wales, Scotland and Northern Ireland, *Oxford Review of Education*, 27, 2

Rahidzab, T., Razidah, I., Janor, R., Ahmed, A. and Aljunid, S. (1999) Programme quality assessment by the implication of variable entry qualifications on students' performance, *Assessment and Evaluation in Higher Education*, 24, 2, 201-210

Rawls, J. (1971) *A Theory of Justice*, Harvard University Press

Read, B., Archer, A. and Leathwood, C. (2003) Challenging Cultures? Student Conceptions of 'Belonging' and 'Isolation' at a Post-1992 University, *Studies in Higher Education*, 28, 3, 261-277

Reay, D., Ball, S. and David, M. (2002) 'It's taking me a long time but I'll get there in the end': mature students on access courses and higher education choice', *British Educational Research Journal*, 28, 1, 5-19

Reay, D., David, M. and Ball, S. (2005) *Degrees of choice: social class, race and gender in higher education*, Stoke on Trent: Trentham

Reay, D., Davies, J., David, M. and Ball, S. (2001) Choices of degree or degrees of choice? Class, 'race' and the higher education choice process, *Sociology,* 35, 4, 855-874

Reddy, P. (2004) *Evaluation of the LHS Year 0 programme in Biology, Optometry, Pharmacy and Psychology*, Aston University

Redmond, P. (2003) *'I just thought it was for people with loads of money.' Experiences and aspirations of widening participation students,* LTSN Research Paper

Rees, G., Fevre, R., Furlong, J. and Gorard, S. (2006) History, place and the learning society: Towards a sociology of lifetime learning, in Lauder, H., Brown, P., Dillabough, J. and Halsey, A. (eds.) *Education, globalization and social change,* Oxford: Oxford University Press

Rees, T. (2001) *Investing in learners: coherence, clarity and equity for student support in Wales*, Cardiff: National Assembly for Wales

Rhodes, C. and Nevill, A. (2004) 'Academic and social integration in higher education: A survey of satisfaction and dissatisfaction within a first year education studies cohort at a new university', *Journal of Further and Higher Education*, 28, 2, 179-193

Rhodes, C., Bill, K., Biscomb, K., Nevill, A. and Bruneau, S. (2002) Widening Participation in Higher Education, *Journal of Vocational Education and Training*, 54, 1, 133-145

Richardson, D. (2003) *The transition to degree level study*, The Higher Education Academy: 4

Richardson, J. and Woodley, A. (2003) Another Look at the Role of Age, Gender and Subject as Predictors of Academic Attainment in Higher Education, *Studies in Higher Education*, 28, 4

Riddell, S., Tinklin, T. and Wilson, A. (2004) *Disabled students and multiple policy innovations in higher education, final report to the Economic and Social and Research Council* (www.ces.ed.ac.uk/PDF per cent20Files/Disability_Report.pdf checked on 15/06/05)

Riddell, S., Wilson, A. and Tinklin, T. (2002) Disability and the wider access agenda: Supporting disabled students in different institutional contexts, *Journal of Widening Participation and Lifelong Learning*, 4, 3, 13-25

Roberts, C., Watkin, M., Oakley, D. and Fox, R. (2003) *Supporting Student Success: What can we learn from the persisters?*, University of Salford: 12

Sanders, C. (2006) Tories: £2bn access drive is a 'failure', *Times Higher Education Supplement*, 28/7/06, p.2

Sanderson, A. (2001) Disabled students in transition: A tale of two sectors' failure to communicate, *Journal of Further and Higher Education*, 25, 2, 227-240

San-Segundo, M. and Valiente, A. (2003) 'Family background and returns to schooling in Spain' *Education Economics*, 11, 1, 39-52

Sargant, N. (2000) *The learning divide revisited*, Leicester: NIACE

Sargant, N. and Aldridge, F. (2002) *Adult learning and social division: a persistent pattern*, Volume 1, Leicester: NIACE

Schuller, T., Raffe, D., Morgan-Klein, B. and Clark, I. (1997) Part-time higher education and the student-employer relationship, *Journal of Education and Work*, 10, 3, 225-236

Sellers, J. and van der Velden, G. (2003) *Supporting Student Retention*, University of Kent at Canterbury: 35

Selwyn, N., Gorard, S. and Furlong, J. (2006) *Adult learning in the digital age,* London: Routledge

Shiner, M. and Modood, T. (2002) 'Help or hindrance? Higher education and the route to ethnic equality' in *British Journal of Sociology of Education* 23, 2, 209-232

Shuttleworth, I., Osborne, B. and Gallagher, T. (2001) *Geographical aspects of participation in Higher Education in Northern Ireland*, (mimeo).

Sinclair, H. and McClements, P. (2004) *An evaluation of the progression of LEAPS students through their first year of Higher Education*, South East of Scotland Wider Access Forum

Singell, L., Waddell, G. and Curs, B. (2005) *Hope for the Pell? The Impact of Merit-Aid on Needy Students*, http://papers.ssrn.com/paper.taf?abstract_id=616783

Sloane, P. and O'Leary, N. (2004) *The Return to a University Education in Great Britain*, Swansea University

Smith, E. and Gorard, S. (2007) Who succeeds in teacher training?, *Research Papers in Education*, (forthcoming)

Smith, J. and Naylor, R. (2001) Determinants of Degree Performance in UK Universities: A statistical analysis of the 1993 Student Cohort, *Oxford Bulletin of Economics and Statistics*, 63, 1, 29-62

Smith, J., McKnight, A. and Naylor, R. (2000) Graduate Employability: Policy, and performance in higher education, *Economic Journal*, 110, 464, F382-411

Smith, K., Rogers, F. and O'Donoghue, E. (2005) Putting students 1st: Overcoming the departmental barriers, in T. Acland, J. Samuel, D. Saunders and J. Storan (eds.) *Access, Retention and Employability: Transforming Higher Education.*, FACE, 115-118

Sutton Trust (2002) *Schools Omnibus 2001-2002 (Wave 8)* A research study among 11-16 year olds on behalf of the Sutton Trust

Sutton Trust (2004) *State school admissions to our leading universities*, mimeo

Taylor, C. and Gorard, S. (2005) *Participation in higher education: Wales, Report for independent study into devolution of the student support system: The Rees Review,* Cardiff: National Assembly for Wales

Taylor, J. and Bedford, T. (2004) Staff perceptions of factors related to non-completion in higher education, *Studies in Higher Education*, 29, 3

Taylor, M. (2004) Widening participation into higher education for disabled students, *Education and Training*, 46, 1, 40-48

Taylor, S. and Spencer, L. (1994) *Individual Commitment to Lifelong Learning: Individual's attitudes.* Report on the qualitative phase, Employment Department

Tett, L. (2004) Mature working-class students in an 'elite' university: Discourses of risk, choice and exclusion, *Studies in the Education of Adults*, 36, 2, 252-264

THES (2006) Labour's student ambitions falter, *Times Higher Education Supplement*, 18/8/06, p.1

Thomas, L. (2002) 'Student retention in higher education: The role of institutional habitus', *Journal of Education Policy*, 17, 4, 423-442

Thomas, L. and Slack, K. (1999) *Evaluation of Aiming High 1999*, Institute for Access Studies, Staffordshire University

Thomas, L. and Slack, K. (2000) *Evaluation of Aiming High 2000*, Institute for Access Studies, Staffordshire University

Thomas, L., Quinn, J., Slack, K. and Casey, L. (2002) *Student services: Effective approaches to retaining students in higher education*, Institute for Access Studies: Staffordshire University.

Thomas, L., Yorke, M. and Woodrow, M. (2001) *Access and retention,* www.actiononaccess. org/resource/aoadocs/ssrep2.doc, checked on 15/06/05

Thomas, W. and Webber, D. (2001) 'Because my friends are': the impact of peer groups on the intention to stay on at sixteen, *Research in Post-Compulsory Education*, 6, 3, 339-354

Thomas, W., Webber, D. and Walton, F. (2003) School effects that shape students' decisions to stay-on in education, *Research in Post-Compulsory Education*, 8, 2, 197-211

Tight, M. (1998) Lifelong learning: opportunity or compulsion?, *British Journal of Educational Studies*, 46, 3, 251-263

Titmus C. (1994) The scope and characteristics of educational provision for adults, in Calder J. (Ed.) *Disaffection and Diversity. Overcoming barriers to adult learning*, London: Falmer

Tooley, J. with Darby, D. (1998) *Educational research: A critique.* London: OFSTED

Tuijnman, A. (1991) Lifelong education: a test of the accumulation hypothesis, *International Journal of Lifelong Learning*, 10, 275-285

Tymms, P., Coe, R. and Merrell, C. (2005) *Standards in English schools: changes since 1997 and the impact of government policies and initiatives*, Report for the *Sunday Times*, http://www.times-archive.co.uk/onlinespecials/english_in_schools.html

UCAS (1999) *Statistical bulletin on widening participation*, Cheltenham: University and Colleges Admissions Service

UCAS (2000) *UCAS News release* 11/10/2000, Cheltenham: University and Colleges Admissions Service

UCAS (2002) *Paving the way,* Cheltenham: UCAS

Ulrich, N. (2004) *Mature students: Access to and experience of HE part-time foreign language degrees,* Aston University

UUK (2001) *Patterns of higher education institutions in the UK* (the Ramsden Report) London: Universities UK

Wakeling, P. (2003) Social class still counts after students reach 21, *Times Higher Education Supplement,* 15th August 2003. Accessed electronically on 29th July 2005

Wakely, K. and Saunders, D. (2004) A Tracking Analysis of Compact Students within Level 1 of their Higher Education Programmes, *Research in Post-Compulsory Education,* 9, 1, 47-62

Walford, G. (2004) No discrimination on the basis of irrelevant qualifications, *Cambridge Journal of Education,* 34, 3, 353-361

Walker, L. (1998) Longitudinal study of drop-out and continuing students who attended the Pre-University Summer School at the University of Glasgow, *International Journal of Lifelong Education,* 18, 3, 217 – 233

Walker, L. (1999) Predicting or guessing: the progress of Scottish Wider Access Programme (SWAP) students at the University of Glasgow. *International Journal of Lifelong Education,* 19, 342-356

Walker, L., Matthew, B. and Black, F. (2004) Widening access and student non-completion: an inevitable link?, *International Journal of Lifelong Education,* 23, 1, 43-59

Wallace, J. (2003) *Supporting the First Year Experience,* London Metropolitan University: 24

Warren, D. (2003) *Improving student retention: A 'team approach',* Annual Conference of the Institute for Learning and Teaching in HE, University of Warwick, Coventry, London Metropolitan University

Watson, D. (2002) *Is UK HE fit for purpose?,* http://www.aua.ac.uk/publications/conference proceedings/2002southampton/david per cent20watson.htm

Watson, D. (2004) Expansion first, equality later, *Times Higher Educational Supplement,* 2/4/04, p.16

Watson, J. and Church, A. (2003) *Funding the future: the attitudes of year 10 pupils in England and Wales to higher education,* London: National Union of Students

Watts, M. and Bridges, D. (2006) The value of non-participation in higher education, *Journal of Education Policy,* 21, 3, 267-290

West, A., Xavier, R. and Hind, A. (2003) *Evaluation of Aimhigher: Survey of Opportunity Bursary Applications 2001/2002: Preliminary Finding, Research Report 497,* London: DfES

Wikipedia (2006) http://en.wikipedia.org/wiki/Higher_education, accessed 4th April 2006

Wilson, F. (1997) The Construction of Paradox? One Case of Mature Students in Higher Education, *Higher Education Quarterly,* 51, 4, 347-366

Wilson, W. (1987) *The Truly Disadvantaged,* Chicago, Chicago University Press

Winn, S. (2002) Student motivation: A socio-economic perspective, *Studies in Higher Education,* 27, 4, 445-457

Wolf, A. (2002) *Does education matter?,* London, Penguin

Wolf, A., Jenkins, A. and Vignoles, A. (2006) Certifying the workforce: economic imperative or failed social policy?, *Journal of Education Policy,* 21, 5, 535-565

Woodrow, M. with Lee, M., McGrane, J., Osborne, B., Pudner, H. and Trotman, C. (1998) *From Elitism to Inclusion: Good practice in widening access to higher education,* London, Universities UK, 155

Woodrow, M., York, M., Lee, M., McGrane, J., Osborne, B., Pudner, H. and Trotman, C. (2002) *Social class and participation: good practice in widening access to higher education*, Universities UK, 183

Yang, B. (1998) Longitudinal study of participation in adult education: a theoretical formulation and empirical investigation, *International Journal of Lifelong Learning*, 17, 4, 247-259

Yorke, M. (1999) *Leaving Early: Undergraduate non-completion in higher education*, London: Falmer Press

Zhou, X., Moen, P. and Tuma, N. (1998) Educational Stratification in Urban China, *Sociology of Education*, 71, 199-222

Index